TALKING AUTISM

VICTORIA HATTON

TALKING Autism
Copyright © 2018 Victoria Hatton
www.autismconsultancyinternational.com

Published by Compass-Publishing 2018
ISBN 978-1-912009-14-5
Printed in the UK by CMP UK

Designed by The Book Refinery Ltd.
www.thebookrefinery.com

A catalogue copy of this book is available from the British Library.
All rights reserved. This book or any portion thereof may not be reproduced or used in any manner whatsoever without the express written permission of the publisher except for the use of brief quotations in a book review.
All links at time of print were valid.

The information contained within this book is provided for information purposes only. Its contents are not intended to amount to advice and you should obtain professional advice before taking or refraining from taking any action as a result of its contents. Victoria disclaims all liability and responsibility arising from any reliance placed on any of the contents of this book. Please note that her professional expertise is that of a teacher, she is not a medical professional and is not a diagnostician.

To Aaron for putting up with me during the many hours this book has taken to write, to my Mum for always believing I could achieve anything and to my Grandad without whom I would never have been able to become a teacher. But most of all to my children, who make me strive every day to be a better version of myself.

Contents

Introduction - Individual approaches for individual children: one size does not fit all 7

Initial Concerns - 11

So, You Think Your Child Could Have Autism? 13
Does a Diagnosis Matter? 15
Girls On The Spectrum 18

The Diagnosis Process - 21

Preparing Yourself For The Diagnostic Process 23
A Diagnosis. What Next? 25
Telling Your Child About Their Diagnosis 29
Telling Friends And Family Members About
Your Child's Diagnosis 32

Getting Educational Support Right For Your Child - 37

Accessing Support And Applying For An Education
Health Care Plan (EHCP) 39
Does My Child Need A Diagnosis Before We Apply
For An EHCP? 42
Creating A Partnership Between Home And School 44

Strategies - 49

Understanding Triggers And Why They Matter 51
Reducing Environmental Triggers 55
Tackling Task Based Triggers 59
Preventing Sensory Overload 62
Raising Self Esteem Whilst Reducing The Fear
Of Making Mistakes 65

The Power Of Special Interests 68
Reducing Demands Without Lowering Expectations 72
Using Schedules To Reduce Meltdowns 77
Getting Out Of The House Without A Meltdown 79
Teaching Friendship Skills 82
Structuring A New Activity.. 85
Helping Your Child To Sleep... 88
Tackling Personal Hygiene 91
Ways To Make Homework Less Stressful.. 94
Revision Tips That Will Make Life A Little Easier............................. 97
The Challenge Of Christmas..100
Preparing A Child To Return To School After The Holidays 103
Helping Children And Young People To Understand Emotions 107
Strategies To Help Young People Who Mask......................................110
Managing Meltdowns 115
Rewards Matter..118
Are Consequences Really Needed?..123

What If School Isn't Working? - 125

Reducing The Risk Of School Refusal 127
Getting Those Who Have Refused School Back
Through The Door 130
Enabling Successful Reintegration After A Period
Of School Refusal Or Exclusion 133
What If School Breaks Down? 136

Final words - 139

What Is It Really Like In Holland?...141
Conclusion - You Matter Too...143
Resources And Further Help 146
About The Author 147

Introduction

INDIVIDUAL APPROACHES FOR INDIVIDUAL CHILDREN: ONE SIZE DOES NOT FIT ALL

Before I get on with the technical part of this book, I want to tell you a short story. Our story...

Nine years ago my world was rocked when my daughter - then age two - was given an Asperger's diagnosis. I was a teacher. I'd done dissertations on Autism. I'd worked with toddlers with Autism all throughout university, and once I'd finished I had taught numerous older children on the Spectrum.

I'd expected the diagnosis. I'd initiated it.

I expected the words but I wasn't prepared for them. But more than that I wasn't prepared for the negativity of the process. The list of things she couldn't do. The lack of ideas about what I should do. The list of places they referred us to that one by one we were turned away from because we didn't fit the criteria. I remember feeling completely and utterly alone. Somehow in my head I had thought that diagnosis would equate to help. That once she had a diagnosis someone would show me how to help her get from A to B. That she would get support in nursery and ultimately in school.

You see from my position as a teacher, I had never realised just how hard it was to get support. Autism was my passion, my background, my life even then. But when it came to my own daughter I found myself second guessing my decisions. Unlike at school I didn't have a team around me to make collective decisions with, I didn't have parents to use a sounding boards... it was just me. And that was scary. Really, really scary.

Within a year of diagnosis, I'd had Skype calls with an expert in Australia and flown out to Peru to see another specialist. The mum inside the teacher needed to know that she had covered her bases, that she was doing all she could to give her daughter the best chance in life. And I appreciate even now the help they gave me, at a time when I didn't know where to turn.

But in reality it wasn't either of those experts who changed our lives. That honour goes to a group of young people who were onboard the Disney Magic Cruise Ship that summer. They got to know my daughter in a way few people ever have - even now remembering it there are tears in my eyes - and they taught her more than anyone else ever has. In the 20 days we spent onboard the cast and characters, taught her how to play, how to trust, how to engage. And they taught me that my daughter would be #UNIQUEANDSUCCESSFUL. They showed me she would be loved. And they taught me that if we want our children to step outside of their comfort zone, sometimes we have to step outside our own.

They made me a better mum. But they also made me a better teacher. You see those experts I went to see, the 100s of books I'd read, they gave me generic strategies - none of which quite fit her or our life. Her Disney friends knew nothing about Autism - they fell in love with a little girl and invented their own ways of helping her - strategies unique to her rather than text book ones.

It's something that whichever young person has walked through the doors of my classroom since then, I've kept in mind. Because the reality is knowing the child in front of you, listening to them and their family is more valuable than any professional knowledge. But when you put the two together, you really can sit back and watch magic happen. From the young man who had spent 4 years out of school, who went back to full time education. To the boy who at 11 couldn't read and write but who telephoned me last week to tell me that he had been accepted to college on the basis of his own handwritten application letter - this combination is something I've never forgotten the value of.

It's why I teach the way I teach, it's why I started writing at Starlight And Stories, it's why I set up my Facebook Group and Autism Consultancy International, and ultimately it's why I am sitting here writing this book. You see, despite the fact that this is a book full of strategies, and things for you to try I want you to always remember that our children are more than a strategy. Often people talk about Autism Strategies, or PDA Strategies. They say that this strategy doesn't work, or that doesn't work. They criticise the child for not learning. Or blame the parents for not parenting.

But the truth is, if we look at what a child is capable of, their interests and strengths and we fit that alongside what feels right to the family, applying personalised strategies to fit the individual, things start to work. And that's what I hope that you will learn from this book. I hope you will gain some strategies, and some ideas to try.

But more than that, I hope it will give you the confidence to tweak these strategies, to make them right for your child, and even to invent some of your own.

Remember always, that you know your child best. So, listen to professionals, take advice, join Facebook groups, talk to other parents and read books like this one. But more than anything trust your own gut reactions, and remember that you can do this.

Take Care,

Victoria x

Initial Concerns

So, You Think Your Child Could Have Autism?

If you are reading this book and wondering where to turn next, wondering whether what you are seeing is just 'normal' childhood behaviour or if something else is contributing you are in the right place. I know it's hard to admit to yourself that a time has come when you need to act on your concerns, but if you've picked up this book then you have come to that conclusion. And I am really proud of you for doing so.

If you take away just one thing, I want it to be this.

You do not have to wait until diagnosis to start taking action.

That process, that piece of paper, does not need to define your journey. You can start taking action today that will change your lives, you don't need to wait for the professionals and waiting lists to catch up with you… because I am going to teach you how. All too often, I see parents beat themselves up because they didn't act sooner. I see families sitting on waiting lists for two years or longer not sure whether to move forward with strategies before they have answers. And I see parents who think that first a diagnosis, and then an EHCP will change their lives for the better.

But I'm going to let you into a secret now. And it's one it takes lots of people much longer to learn:

If we want our children to cope better in the world we often have to be the first ones to change.

It doesn't mean you're a bad parent. On the contrary, if you've got this far you're obviously a pretty awesome one. But what it does mean, is it's time to put those strategies into practice, and not just once or twice but every single day. Consistently. Because if you want an easy life, first it's going to get hard. Really hard. But let me tell you something. You can do this. I believe in you. You can make changes… and not only changes that work for your child but ones that work for your family. How do I know? Because I have been there. And I've helped 100s of families do exactly that.

And I want to help you as well.

So whilst you're reading this book make sure you join our free Facebook Group #UNIQUEANDSUCCESSFUL: The Community so that if you have any questions or don't understand anything I've written you can get clarification when you need it.

Does a Diagnosis Matter?

Whilst I understand that there are those that worry that too much labelling is a bad thing, for me labels matter. They matter a lot. I understand that in principle the education system works on need, not diagnosis. I also understand that a label travels with a child into adulthood, and I know that in itself can have implications. Both of those factors should be considered.

I am not by any means suggesting that we should label everyone. A diagnostic process is essential to ensure that the right children receive labels at the right time. It's also essential to ensure that those areas of development in which a child is struggling, can't with intervention be resolved. However, what I *am* saying is that if you have concerns, you should investigate them further.

Labels matter to children more than you know

As an undiagnosed Dyslexic until I was fifteen I know firsthand the feelings of inadequacy, of frustration, of feeling as though I was a failure. I could not understand why no matter how hard I tried my spelling was atrocious and my handwriting was worse. My teenage brain simply thought I was stupid because homework took me so much longer than my peers.

A diagnosis did not change the support I got in school. It did however change the way I viewed myself. Overnight I had a tribe. A clan. I researched strategies, but more than anything I became less frustrated. Three years later I passed A Level English at Grade A, before going onto read English at Cambridge University. Without a diagnosis, I'm not sure I would have believed in myself enough to apply. And I'm sure I wouldn't have had the confidence to argue with such passion in my interview. I went from being someone, who had always believed they couldn't, to someone who believed they could. Not knowing was far more painful than knowing.

But they also matter to you as a parent

As a parent a label means that you are not going mad, and that you are not alone. They also mean you have a battering ram with which to get others to listen (which sometimes works, and sometimes doesn't).

In the early days, before my daughter's diagnosis, her nursery's very limited (read non-existent) knowledge of Autism in girls meant that they were insistent that her difficulties were because she was an only child. And perhaps with hindsight to some degree siblings would have helped. They would have softened some of the edges, she may have been more used to hustle and bustle. But being an only child was not the cause of her Meltdowns, nor was it the cause of her anxiety.

She has never qualified for additional help at school. But I know her diagnosis has affected both the strategies we use at home to tackle problems and the strategies her excellent teachers have used too.

Without a diagnosis I would have been working in the dark, especially in the early days. She was too young for CAMHs (Child and Adolescent Mental Health Services) and 'too able' for SEND (Special Educational Needs And Disability) groups. She was an anomaly, mostly because most girls are diagnosed far later. Books and the internet became my sources, The only way I had to help her. Without a diagnosis, and the early intervention that meant I could give her, our lives would look very different. At the very least I would have spent more time stumbling around, and worried.

And yes... even to teachers

They matter because whilst in theory the system works on need, it works a whole lot faster with diagnostic evidence to back up that need. But even more importantly, diagnoses act as a signpost. When I walk into a new class, I instantly know that x is likely to find change difficult or that y will struggle to sit through a whole lesson. Labels make me more patient and less frustrated.

They make me a better teacher and in a world where everything, especially in education moves fast, they make me a more efficient one. They mean I know where to start looking for strategies. And although for most students those strategies will need to be altered and adjusted for them as an individual, it gives me a base to work from. In areas I'm not a specialist in that matters.

Especially today where a lack of resources can often mean access to specialist teachers and educational psychologists is minimal, that's important.

If you've never been different and not known why, you'll never fully understand how important it is. But believe me it is. Explained in the right way it can be a positive. Deciding to pursue a diagnosis is never an easy decision. But it may just be the greatest gift you ever give your child.

You see a label is more than a name. It is the gift of understanding. The gift of a Tribe.

Girls On The Spectrum

What seems like a lifetime ago, I sat down at a computer not unlike the one I sit typing this book on and searched 'Girls with Autism'. It was that search and an article written by Tony Attwood, who back then was one of the few professionals tackling the fact that girls on the Spectrum often present differently to their male counterparts that made me pursue a diagnosis for my daughter.

I still remember sitting and reading it, and just how much everything he said resonated with what I was seeing in my own home. Yet still almost nine years later I'm acutely aware that so many professionals don't make these distinctions and recognise just how differently Autism can present in girls. As I walk through my daily life, I come across girls who are without doubt on the Spectrum. Undiagnosed girls with Autism who have often accessed PRUs, specialist schools and uncountable professionals. Girls and young women who should have been diagnosed long before their path crosses mine. These girls are not hidden. They are there and very much in the system. But the truth is that all too often professionals simply do not know what to look for.

So here is my guide for things that you as a parent should flag up to professionals who are considering whether to refer for a diagnostic assessment. Please note however, that this list is not intended as confirmation of diagnosis, rather as a list which suggests that further advice should be sought by specialist professionals.

Girls with Autism may:

→ **Find change difficult**

They may withdraw, refuse to go to school, shut down or become confrontational if changes to their normal routine occur. This can include theoretically positive changes, such as an outing as well as less preferred activities such as the cancellation of a favourite TV-show.

- **Like to be pre-warned if things are going to be different**

    Even with this warning they will often become anxious about the change. They will often ask multiple questions until they are sure about how it will affect them.

- **Find friendships challenging**

    They may have friends but are likely to try to dominate the friendship, perhaps by talking about the same topic or by wanting to play the same game in the same way. They are likely to struggle with the nuances of social communication and become distressed if things go wrong within the friendship because they are unsure how to fix them.

- **Have very fixed ideas**

    And find it difficult if someone else disagrees with those ideas. A normally extremely well behaved child could for example start adamantly disagreeing with the teacher if they feel that something is wrong.

- **Present very differently at home and at school**

    Many children on the Spectrum mask their anxieties at school either out of fear of getting in trouble for not conforming to the norm, or out of a desire to appeal 'normal' in front of friends. When they arrive home their feelings of anxiety which have built up during the day can then explode, leaving parents struggling to cope. Others cope well in the relatively low pressure environment of home, but struggle to cope in a busy school environment which is full of demands.

- **Outwardly look very neurotypical**

    Reports suggest that girls on the Spectrum are often particularly adept at mimicking the behaviour of peers, without necessarily understanding the reasons for that behaviour. Many are very difficult to diagnose on initial assessment because of this, and are likely to need their behaviour observing over an extended period of time by someone with experience in diagnosing girls.

- **Be desperate to fit in**

    And almost try too hard to be part of the group yet never really succeed.

- **Or withdraw and isolate themselves during social times**

    Perhaps choosing to read a book or talk to a member of staff at school instead of their peers.

- **Have similar interests to their peers**

    Animals, Disney, Harry Potter and particular TV shows are all common special interests for girls on the Spectrum. Their passion for their subject of interest is likely to be more intense than that of their peers however and may dominate many of their conversations.

- **Struggle to do well in school during times of anxiety**

    This is especially common when they perceive they are being tested. They may struggle to answer questions verbally under pressure and crumble during written tests despite normally performing well.

- **Use avoidance strategies**

    These can include saying that they feel unwell, if put under pressure. This may be done consciously as a deliberate attempt to escape a difficult situation. Or her anxiety levels may be so extreme that she genuinely feels ill.

This list isn't exhaustive, and most girls will not display all of the characteristics above. I would also like to remind you that I'm not a diagnostician, just a mum and a teacher who has met and worked with many girls on the Spectrum. Someone who thinks it's time that our girls got the support they need when they are young enough for it to make a difference.

My hope is that this chapter will help to make sure that professionals listen to your concerns, feel free to use it as a battering ram if you so wish.

The Diagnosis Process

Preparing Yourself For The Diagnostic Process

Navigating the SEND world is not an easy journey. It's complex at the best of times. But in the current political climate with reducing funds and increasing waiting lists it's more important than ever that parents are informed. Diagnosis can be a difficult journey. Both emotionally and practically. But it is important before you begin the process that you realise that a diagnosis does not necessarily equate to support - and likewise your child should be given access to the support they need regardless of where they are in the diagnostic procedure.

A diagnosis comes from health, whereas support – educational support at least – is decided by Education. They will battle with each other about both practical and financial responsibility, often at the expense of the child. It saddens me to say this, but you cannot assume that the system wants what is best for your child. You need to take control, as a parent you have more power than you realise, and your knowledge (or lack of it) will without a doubt impact on the level of support your child receives and how long it takes them to access that support.

This chapter is written from my combined knowledge as the mother of a daughter with Asperger's Syndrome and as a teacher in a specialist unit for children with Autism. It is not a magic wand, it will neither guarantee you a diagnosis or support, but hopefully it will ease the process a little, leaving you with enough strength to fight the battles that will come your way.

If you are worried about your child's development in any way you have two possible routes you can take. Your GP can refer you for diagnosis and so can your child's nursery/ school. The systems will eventually converge but as an initial contact both are equally effective. It can really help to take a written list of your concerns with you to the meeting. If you can video the behaviours that are worrying you and/ or take statements with you from any professionals (or other people that might be seen as objective) this can also speed up the process.

It hasn't escaped my notice over the years, that I am listened to far more often when I wear my teacher hat than when I wear my mum hat. It's wrong, but it's true. If one set of professionals don't listen to you, try the next set. If neither takes your concerns seriously it can help to talk to them about how the things you are worried about fit into the triad of impairments that make up Autism. This can be especially important if you are the parent of a girl, as girls often present differently to the standard diagnostic criteria. As rubbish as it is, neither GPs nor teachers receive formal training in Autism.

By the time you get to the appointment it's likely (however scary this thought is) that you will know at least as much about Autism as they do. If you still don't get answers, or get the all too common 'see how things go' response, you can choose to go down the route of a private diagnosis. The National Autistic Society helpline has a list of people (at various prices) in each area who are able to carry this out. It's important to add here, that a private diagnosis may not be recognised, either by health or education. It can however help to provide you as a family with answers and it can often be used as an effective battering ram to force the system into carrying out the diagnostic procedure. As early intervention is key, this can be a valuable time saving tool.

The diagnostic procedure can take a long time. It isn't an overnight process. Depending on the area where you live current waiting times for the wheels of the system to begin churning can be anything between six months and two years. Unfortunately there is very little you can do to speed this up. However, it's worth mentioning that educational support is technically based upon need not diagnosis. Therefore if you can argue that your child needs additional help at school they shouldn't have to wait until after diagnosis is complete.

During the assessment period multiple people are likely to be involved. These may include (but are not limited to) a clinical psychologist, an educational psychologist, a paediatrician, a speech and language therapist and an Autism specialist teacher. The people involved will be experts in diagnosis, but not necessarily in intervention. Be aware that even if you leave the process with a diagnosis and a list of your child's difficulties you are unlikely to leave with a plan of action.

But that doesn't mean that you as a parent can't form one.

A Diagnosis. What Next?

The moment we received our diagnosis is still etched in my brain. We were told my daughter had Autism one moment and the next we were ushered out of the room. I remember standing in the car park at the child development centre, wondering what on earth I was supposed to do next. And I remember my mum looking at me and saying, thank goodness you know what you're doing imagine what it must be like for parents who haven't even heard of Autism.

At that moment I didn't feel like I knew what I was doing, despite my years of professional knowledge. I felt shellshocked and alone. So please know that if you have picked up this book just after a diagnosis, you are not alone. There are a Tribe of us, and we're a pretty cool Tribe too.

Before you embark on the strategies and implementing new things, I want you to go and get yourself a cup of tea and really concentrate on this chapter. Because you matter too. Anything you implement from now on, relies upon you and the more you take care of you, the better you will be able to help your child as you navigate this strange new world you have found yourself in.

Breathe

Diagnosis brings about a complex mix of feelings, worries and emotions, some will be shared, others unique to you. Remember it's ok to give yourself the time and space to feel however you need to feel.

I remember only too well, the cacophony of emotions which overwhelmed me eight years ago. For me it was a mixture of relief that at last I understood, terror that my daughter would never have a friend and guilt that I was letting her down because I didn't know how to help her.

But however you feel, remember that that is ok. Breathe and remember that you are human.

Enjoy them

Take time amidst the panic to enjoy your child exactly as they are.

Remember that they are the same person today as they were yesterday, no more, no less. Spend some time just playing or talking with them about the things they love. Remind yourself that together you are a formidable force.

Find a Tribe

If there is one regret I have from our early days after diagnosis, it's that I isolated us both. I found it hard to be around families who had neurotypical children and yet when we went to local support groups, it was rare to find others of a similar age and profile. It took us a long time to find our Tribe: both the friends with neurotypical children who didn't take no for an answer, and those we have found online.

It makes a difference. A huge one

However hard it is to put yourself out there and find that Tribe, I promise it is worth it. Not only for you, but for your child. The National Autistic Society keep a list of local support groups, you can find details either through their website or by calling their helpline. But if leaving the house is often challenging it's also worth taking a look at the many fantastic Facebook support groups out there. As an added bonus Facebook never sleeps, so the answers to your questions are always waiting.

Listen to (and ask for) advice

Don't be afraid to ask for advice and listen to what is given. Whether you have professionals involved or speak to other parents who have travelled the path before, listening to others is a great way to find strategies that work. And believe me sometimes it's the crazy ideas that work the best…. I have been known to spend significant amounts of time pretending to be a blue cat in order to engage with a student… if it feels right it's probably worth a try.

Do your research (Or find someone who has)

Read, read and read some more. Whether it's via books, blog posts or our #UNIQUEANDSUCCESSFUL Membership scheme empower yourself. Learn everything you can. Doing so will not only put you in the best possible position to understand your child but it will also empower you. It will mean you feel more confident in your parenting decisions and are better placed to fight for what your child needs.

But follow your gut...

There is a plethora of advice out there. Some good and some not so good. If it doesn't sound right, feels too good to be true, or offers a miracle cure it's probably best avoided. Remember always that your child is your child, unique and individual. You know them best. You have the final call. Follow your instincts and you will not go far wrong.

Ditch the guilt

Yes I know, I hear you. It's hard. Guilt comes with the territory of being a parent. But listen to me now and listen carefully. You are a human being doing their very best. No one can ask more of you than that. I know right now it feels like you are in this way out of your depth, but I promise you it will get easier.

Find out about local services

Investigate what is available to you locally, whether that's local Autism support groups or access to speech therapy, occupational therapy or educational support. Depending on where you're based your entitlement to local services will vary, but in many areas it pays to do your research. All too often services exist that families are never openly told about.

Get ready to stand your ground

The hardest part of this journey is going to be getting the right support, which doesn't happen easily. To secure the best future for your child, you are going to have to get pushy. You're going to have to fight. Prepare yourself for this right from the beginning. Don't assume because one person tells you something it is right, check and double check. Then fight some more. As hard as it is to say this, sadly the children who get access to services are those whose parents fight for those services.

Remember, things will get easier

Right now things feel completely overwhelming, you are not sure where to turn for help and your roadmap feels as though it has disappeared. It won't always be this way. Over time you will grow more confident, you will begin to devise a new roadmap, and a new kind of normal will develop. You, your child and your family will be happy. You can do this, and if you need our help we are here to help you to do so. This book will hopefully get you started on that journey.

Telling Your Child About Their Diagnosis

I believe strongly that children have the right to know their diagnosis, in an age appropriate way, from a very young age. In fact telling your child about their diagnosis is one of the most important things you will ever do. I know that telling them isn't easy; finding the right moment can be hard. And I also know that if you have reached that stage then you are probably worrying about how your child will react.

But the reality is, that children almost always react far more positively than you expect. From a very young age our children realise that they are different. A diagnosis is a way of explaining the difference to them, of helping them to process it, to understand that they are not alone.

Put simply, knowing their diagnosis will help their self esteem, it will give them the chance to be part of a Tribe and it will enable them to discuss with you more easily the things that they find hard.

So, how can you help them understand?

- ✓ Talk about how being different is a good thing, about how in our own way we are all different, both in terms of our physical differences, our interests and the way our brains work. Remind them that if we were all the same the world would be very boring.
- ✓ Remember that children with Autism deal in facts. Explain to them in an age appropriate way why Autism means that they find some things harder than their peers, but also why it's a good thing that gives them advantages as well as difficulties.
- ✓ Do a quick Google search to find famous people who are on the Spectrum or who are thought to have been on the Spectrum. Tailor the list to people whose accomplishments will appeal to your child and show them just what it is possible to achieve with Autism.

- ✓ Show them their own achievements and what they can do when they put their mind to it. Focus on whatever it is they excel at, even if that is something that traditionally wouldn't be seen as an achievement: whether that is being exceptional at Minecraft creations or knowing every fact there is to know about Pokemon it matters.

- ✓ Explain why it's important to work on the things we are brilliant at and how, if we continue to work at the things we find hard, we can excel even further at the things we are good at.

Why shouldn't you keep it a secret?

The longer you keep a diagnosis a secret for, the bigger the deal it becomes. When you tell your child it therefore becomes bigger to them. The earlier they know the smaller it seems, a diagnosis is just a natural part of life, nothing to be scared of or worried about….. in the words of my daughter when a friend asked her what it was like to have Autism:

"*I have no idea, I've always had Autism… what is it like to not have Autism?*"

She is proud to be Autistic. And when asked the other day whether she wishes some things were easier, like for instance the fact that her anxiety levels often get in the way of things she would love to do, she replied quite simply:

"*No, because then I wouldn't be me.*"

Autism as a diagnosis doesn't feel big to her, because she has always known, and because we take time to stress the positives, and to point out Autistic adults on a regular basis who are #UNIQUEANDSUCCESSFUL.

Being different is hard as a child. Really hard. But what you need to remember is that it isn't the diagnosis that makes them different, it's the way their brain works. If you avoid telling them they feel different, but don't have the answers about why. Understanding their diagnosis means that it's more likely that they will be able to talk openly to you, without feeling like they need to protect you from their worries.

Knowing their diagnosis can be a huge positive. It can give your child a Tribe. It can give them understanding. But most of all it can make them feel less alone. I cannot tell you when the right time for telling your child about their diagnosis is. That is a decision for you and your family. But I can tell you that not knowing can be incredibly hard.

Telling Friends And Family Members About Your Child's Diagnosis

Talking to friends and family about your child's diagnosis is something that many people worry about just how to approach. And the media's portrayal of Autism's extremes often don't help. After all most of our children don't resemble Rain Man in the slightest, and if you're reading this book my guess is that your children are also probably verbal and therefore don't fit into the non-verbal stereotype that many associate with Autism.

A Tribe is important and friends and family are an important part of that the Tribe. The ones who matter will be there for you no matter what the future holds, and it will be easier for them to understand the unpredictability of your life and reluctance to commit to certain activities if they know about your child's diagnosis. I would be lying to you, if I didn't say here and now that some will fall by the wayside. Our lives are often wonderful, full of the love and excitement that our children bring. But there are also lows - times when we let people we care about down, and times when quite frankly we don't have the energy to think about them at all. It takes a special kind of friend to stick around.

I am under no illusion that the friends I have lost over the years, haven't disappeared because of my daughter or her diagnosis, but because of me and the kind of friend that I have been able to be to them. In most cases they made far more effort than I did to stay in touch, I just didn't have the resilience at the time to be a part of their lives. The reality is that it is hard to be surrounded by children playing beautifully together when you are not sure whether your child will ever walk through the door without having a Meltdown. And listening to the worries of parents of neurotypical children often feels somewhat inane. My friends and family didn't change when we got a diagnosis but I did. I became more focused, more direct and definitely less patient. Above all I realised that if a friendship caused either my daughter or I more stress than pleasure it probably wasn't one I was going to retain.

Those who stay around for the long haul, have your back in a way that prior to this diagnosis you never dreamt you would need. Those who don't often just need something different than we are able to give in a world where we are already giving our all. For me, they were three friends from university, all in different areas of the country. Friends I rarely make the effort to contact, but ones I know nevertheless would be there for me in a heartbeat if I needed them.

Anyway I digress somewhat...

If you have decided to talk to your friends and family how do you explain what you and your child need them to know? How do you explain this thing called Autism…

The short technical answer is that what connects children with Autism is a common difficulty with social communication and interaction. They will also in their own way display behaviours, activities and interests which are repetitive and restricted.

In addition to this if your child has a diagnosis of Pathological Demand Avoidance they may also experience high degrees of anxiety if any demands are placed on them.

So in terms of friends and family what does this mean in practical terms. And what can you tell them so that they really understand:

- **'Bad behaviour' is often a way of communicating when something is wrong**

    It may be their way of telling you that they are anxious, feeling sensory overwhelm or just simply the only way they know of telling you that they can't cope. After all, if you have social and communication difficulties it can be hard to put into words how you are feeling, especially when you are upset.

- **When they push you away the hardest, it's often the time they need you the most**

    When children with Autism enter crisis they often exhibit what is known as the flight or fight mode. This doesn't mean that they don't care about those they run from or lash out at, in fact often those in the firing line are those they care the most about. It just means they haven't yet learnt the way to regulate how they feel and to tell you when things have become too overwhelming.

→ **Just because they appear calm on the surface doesn't mean that is how they feel on the inside**

Often children on the Spectrum seem to go from 0 to 100 in a matter of seconds. In reality, they are often holding things together in difficult circumstances all through the day. The final straw may be something very small, but the culmination of all the small things that happen during the day can just mean that eventually things become too much. All too often looking fine doesn't mean feeling fine.

→ **If they can't do a task today that they managed yesterday it doesn't mean that they are trying to be difficult**

Children with Autism often perform differently at different times and on different days. Their ability to concentrate on a task often depends on external factors, like the environment they are working in, the time of day, the amount of sleep they got the night before and how anxious they feel about what is coming next. If you get the environment right and help them to manage their anxiety, you will go a long way to help them be able to perform more consistently.

→ **You are scary when you don't smile**

For children who find facial expressions and emotions hard to read, there is nothing more worrying than a non-smiling adult. All too often even a neutral face will make them feel anxious. It will be interpreted as anger, as frustration or as indifference. They will then struggle to concentrate on anything else, whilst they worry about what they have done to make you feel that way.

→ **Change to their routine is unimaginably hard, especially if that change is unplanned**

Children with Autism often rely on routine and predictability to regulate their world and to ground them. Changing that routine can be incredibly unsettling and can mean that their emotions become too big to handle. Using schedules to help prepare them for change can help to reduce anxiety, it can act as a visual reminder that although some things have changed other things in their life will remain the same.

→ **A sanction shouldn't ever be given during a Meltdown**

I'm a firm believer of both rewards and consequences. The real world operates on both, and both used properly can make a difference to all children and their ability to learn how to cope in a world which isn't always suited to their needs. That said both should be used carefully and with kindness. No matter what has happened, a Meltdown is not the time to talk about sanctions. It can wait. They should be discussed afterwards once the child is calm.

→ **Having more control can make it easier to do what needs to be done - especially for children with Pathological Demand Avoidance**

Feeling as though you have no control over what is happening is a scary prospect for any of us. For a child with Pathological Demand Avoidance it can quickly lead to a downward spiral of anxiety. Finding ways to give them more control is often the best way to make them feel more able to meet your demands. Thinking carefully about how you ask for things to be done and building in choices can make a huge difference.

→ **When everyone in their lives work together it can make an enormous difference**

Children with Autism benefit massively from consistency. When their parents, family members and teachers are on the same page and use the same strategies it can make a huge difference. Parents know their children the best and are all too often dismissed by others in the family and professionals. Getting it right will improve outcomes for children.

→ **Anxiety is a very real factor, to the extent that for some children it can make them feel (and even be) physically ill**

Focusing on looking at triggers and reducing anxiety levels will have a huge impact on the lives of children with Autism. Anxiety is not a peripheral issue to be dealt with later, once behaviour and learning have been figured out. Helping a child to manage their anxiety and reducing that anxiety is key to enabling them to learn and to manage their behaviour. It's important that friends and family members don't judge the order in which parents decide to tackle the battles which need to be fought.

→ **Just because they might not always score well in standardised tests, it doesn't mean they can't change the world**

Children with Autism are often specialists rather than generalists. School based tests can be hard for them, questions are often not written literally, performing in timed conditions increases anxiety, and tests aren't made on their specialist subjects. Focusing on what they can do, listening to them talk about their special interests and reminding them of just how brilliant they are is just as important as helping them catch up in the areas they struggle. Self esteem matters. Intelligence isn't always the score on a test. And success isn't always measured on paper.

The key is to be honest with your family and friends. Be realistic about the challenges, but don't forget to share the positives. Together you will make a formidable force for your children.

Getting Educational Support Right For Your Child

Accessing Support And Applying For An Education Health Care Plan (EHCP)

Unfortunately once you have a diagnosis it does not necessarily equate to additional help either at home or at school. The help your child does get will be determined by the policy of the individual health and education authorities in which you live. Again, it's wrong but true. Help often comes down to a postcode lottery.

When it comes to services provided by health, I have limited knowledge. Except to say that usually the families that get access to services are those that complain the loudest.

Waiting lists post diagnosis, can and do move. You will however have to be very persistent.

Clinical psychologists and speech therapists are both varied in terms of their Autism knowledge. Talking to local parents can help to determine which ones in the area are likely to be the most helpful to your child and it's often worth waiting longer to see someone skilled than it is to see someone with less expertise.

When it comes to education it can help to ask to see the policy of support for students with Autism from your local education authority. This should be available as a public document and will allow you to match your child's needs with the level of support they are currently getting. If they have been receiving support prior to diagnosis, the authority may have used an SEBD (Social Emotional and Behavioural Difficulties) checklist initially, so will need to switch to the Autism one post diagnosis. This is usually a good thing as it often leads to more appropriate support.

Most students in mainstream schools will not qualify for an EHCP, but this does not mean the school doesn't have to give them support. This document is your best tool for ensuring they get the support they need and are assessed for an EHCP when they meet the threshold. In our authority in order for a school to apply for an EHCP they must already be putting in 17 hours of 1:1 support per week. If they aren't doing this it's likely the request will be knocked back. Don't let this put you off though, with enough pressure from you that needn't be the case.

It's worth knowing that it isn't just schools that can apply for the process to be started. As a parent you are within your rights to ring the LEA and ask them to start the assessment yourself. If you do this it's worth letting the school know that is your intention so they can look out for the paperwork the authority sends. Without doing this in bigger schools it can easily go astray, leading to further delays in the process.

Do not assume that the teacher you are dealing with understands the EHCP or funding process. Most don't. It isn't something that they do regularly and it's not something they are trained in. It's worth asking if your LEA have an 'Autism Team', a bank of specialist teachers who can come in and provide support. They often liaise regularly with the authority about provision and can help the school to word the paperwork appropriately and ensure the application includes all the relevant evidence. Their report will also carry significantly more weight than that of teachers working in the school.

Unfortunately in the current climate, many of these teams now need to be bought in by the school. So it may take a little pushing to encourage the school to seek the help they need. Once the paperwork goes off to the authority, it's well worth chasing and checking on it on a regular basis. Paperwork goes missing, doesn't get opened and lands on the wrong person's desk all too regularly. If the officers know you are on the ball and will be chasing them, they are more likely to be more efficient. Again, it's wrong but it's true. Authorities just like schools are massively overstretched and there simply aren't enough people to do the work. The people who get access to services are the ones who demand it.

If your child gets granted an EHCP it will come with a level of funding attached to it, which is rarely enough to meet their true needs. What parents and teachers don't know is that this amount is not fixed in stone. The school can and should negotiate - though again many do not realise that they have the power to do this. If you look back at the support policy I talked about earlier, it should contain funding ranges. These ranges should equate your child's needs, the support they should get and the level of funding they need. If the school feels they can't provide the support a child needs with the funding they are being given they can ask for this to be changed at any annual review. It's important to note here, that an annual review can be requested at any time, either by the school or by you as a parent.

Submitting an educational psychologist's report and a report from the Autism team in support of this is usually expected, though not always essential. Once this request has been sent into the authority, it's again likely that both you and the school will need to chase. Parents have real power with authorities. They know they aren't providing the service they should – as do schools – and often as uncomfortable as it is, parental pressure is the only way to get them to do so.

Does My Child Need A Diagnosis Before We Apply For An EHCP?

One question that I am often asked by parents is whether it's necessary to have a diagnosis *before applying for an EHCP.*

My answer in no uncertain terms, is no. There is no need to have a diagnosis prior to starting the EHCP process. Support is dependent on need not on diagnosis. There are many children with a diagnosis who will never receive additional support, likewise there are others who will not fulfil the full diagnostic criteria but who will be eligible for additional support.

The only difference is that students without a diagnosis will be assessed by the criteria for those young people with Social Emotional And Behavioural Difficulties, rather than on the Autism framework. It's also highly unlikely that you would be able to get an Autism specific school named on the EHCP.

But for the vast majority of students the difference a diagnosis will make to the level of support they are entitled to via an EHCP will be negligible. There is therefore no reason to wait until diagnosis is complete or even begun to begin the process.

How do you start the process of applying without a diagnosis?

The first course of action should be to speak to your child's school, they will be able to advise you on the criteria for applying for an EHCP in your area, and the likelihood of your child qualifying for support. The threshold seems to get increasingly high as the budget cuts bite, so be aware that even if your child is finding school hard they may not qualify for external funding. In many authorities schools are expected to find the first 17 hours of 1:1 funding themselves before the LEA will commit extra funding.

If you feel that your child meets the criteria but school are reluctant to apply you can apply to the LEA directly to assess your child for an EHCP. Your local Parent Partnership service should be able to guide you on the local procedures for this. Please be aware however that if an assessment is unsuccessful in most authorities you will have to wait six months before reapplying.

What information will the LEA require during the process?

Whilst the exact requirements will vary to some degree from area to area, you should expect the local authority to ask for a paper trail spanning at least six months. They will want to know what additional needs your child has and what support is currently being given by school and other authorities in order to meet those needs. The more evidence you and school can provide, the stronger your case will be. Any reports written by professionals about your child will be taken into account, so if for example you have visited your GP to discuss their anxiety then a report from them will prove useful.

Most authorities will require reports from Educational Psychologists and Specialist Teacher, as well as reports from school staff and parents. Even if you aren't successful in getting an EHCP these reports can provide useful suggestions for things that could be done differently to support your child, and be used to show a history of difficulty in future applications.

How likely is my child to get an EHCP if they are not behind their peers academically?

There are two main reasons that LEAs award EHCPs the first is if a child's academic levels are significantly lower than their peers, the second is if they are causing a significant disruption to learning. How the individual LEA determines that varies. Whilst it isn't unheard of for a child or young person to get an EHCP on the grounds of anxiety it is extremely difficult and would require significantly more evidence. The same would apply to any child who masks. In my experience those students most likely to be awarded an EHCP on this basis have usually spent a great deal of time out of school prior to it happening.

The thresholds for EHCPs are high. So if you decide to apply, go in armed with everything you have and be prepared for a battle.

Creating A Partnership Between Home And School

As much as many children and young people with Autism like to try to divide their lives into manageable chunks, the reality is that when it comes to the relationship between school and home it simply isn't possible to do so.

What happens at school impacts on home, and what happens at home impacts on school. It's inevitable that the two will cross over.

As many children struggle to talk about the other world they inhabit when in one place, it's crucial that the adults involved in their lives work together to ensure the best outcomes.

What can you do to build a good relationship with your child's teachers?

Over my teaching career which has spanned over fifteen years I've come across many parents. Some of whom I remember with great fondness and others who challenged me far more than their children did.

Ultimately just like children, adults work better with those who they feel respect and like them, so here are my top five tips for working with teachers.

- → **Teachers are human too**

    Remember that although your child is the most important thing in your world, the teacher has the needs of 30+ children they need to juggle. This doesn't mean that they care any less about them as individuals, but it does mean that because they are human sometimes they forget things. I really appreciate it when parents write things down for me as well as tell me verbally, it helps me to make sure that I get it right.

- → **Remember, they have a life outside school**

    Please ring to make an appointment if you would like to speak to a member of staff. There is nothing more difficult to manage than a parent turning up at school demanding to see a teacher now. If it's during the day it means a class full of students are unsettled by their teacher leaving - and we all know how difficult unexpected change can be for some children. If it's at the end of the day, things can be just as tricky to negotiate. I'm usually in work by seven in the morning and try to leave as soon as I can at the end of the day. I do my classroom preparation in the morning because at night I need to pick my children up from childcare. I can usually rearrange things with 24 hours notice, but need that time to make sure that my family are ok. That said, if it is genuinely urgent, calling the office and saying something like "I know Mrs Z is really busy, but I'm worried about my child, could you possibly ask if she can call me back as soon as possible" will mean you get a call back as soon as is humanly possible and unless a complete disaster occurs always within the same day.

→ **Keep in mind that our children do not always interpret things correctly.**

Try to avoid getting confrontational until you have heard both sides of the story. It doesn't mean your child is lying, they almost certainly genuinely believe their version of events but they can interpret things differently. Take for instance the student who many years ago went home distressed because she was convinced a girl in her class hated her. She told her mum that the girl was a bully who was always staring at her and being mean to her. She was right the girl always looked as though she was staring because she had an eye condition which made her look that way. The two girls had never spoken. The student had just assumed that because she only stared at people when she was angry with them, that that was what was motivating the other child. Starting the dialogue with "X came home last night and thinks that x happened, can you try to find out if he has interpreted it properly please" is much more likely to result in a full investigation and a positive meeting than going in angrily because you think your child has been bullied. They may have

45

been and it should be looked into, but there is also the possibility that the event has been misinterpreted.

- **Say thank you**

    I can count on one hand the number of times parents have thanked me when I have gone out of my way for their child. And that is understandable, I am 'just' doing my job and parents are busy. But the truth is when a teacher goes above and beyond by creating special resources, or by giving a student extra time they are often doing it at the expense of time with their own children. A simple thank you goes a very long way to making a teacher feel appreciated. A handwritten card at Christmas or the end of the year, is something that will be treasured forever. It's no exaggeration to say that I still have a letter sent by a parent in my first year of teaching, telling me the difference I made to his daughter. If ever I'm having a bad day, reading that letter makes me remember why I give my all every day to every student.

- **Encourage openness**

    Tell your child's teacher that you are happy for them to be open with you if your child finds something difficult or has a bad day. Tell them you know they can be challenging at times and that you want to help in whatever way you can. Knowing that you want to work together is a great start to any relationship.

- **What if the relationship just isn't working?**

    I more than most know how frustrating it can be when it feels as though school isn't listening to you about your own child. I go into a meeting as a professional and people take onboard every recommendation I make about the children I teach. When I go to a meeting about my daughter it's often a very different story. After all when it comes to her, I am 'just' a mum.

Over the years I've developed coping strategies to help me a) not lose the plot and b) not look like the neurotic mother you are often made to feel like. After all, however upset I am when I don't feel listened to or respected I know that for the sake of my daughter I have to keep calm. The first of these strategies is to have a ready supply of chocolate for my own personal consumption, the rest are below.

My top tips for trying to rebuild relationships with school staff, even if they haven't always been positive:

→ **Keep in mind that teacher training is lacking in key areas**

Remember that teachers are given no formal Autism training, they are also given no formal training in dealing with parents. Despite this they feel as though they should know what they are doing. When you come along with more knowledge and understanding, it can be difficult for them to admit that they don't really know what they are doing.

→ **Keep it positive**

Enter the meeting with a positive spirit - I know it's easier said than done, but if you start it in a negative way it's hard to change the tone half way through.

→ **Give them constructive ways they can help**

I honestly believe that almost all teachers do want to help, giving them constructive ways they can do so, especially if they don't add to their workload will usually be taken onboard. If you feel as though both you and they have run out of ideas and your child has a diagnosis, they should have access to a local Autism team that they can call in to help.

→ **Give them something concrete**

Try to keep a log of data, this will help you feel more in control and also helps to take some of the emotion out on both sides. You can for instance by tracking and realising that your child comes home from school upset on a Tuesday and a Thursday, go to school armed with that. And say, 'I've been trying to work out why X finds Tuesdays and Thursdays so difficult, can we work together to try to figure it out.'

- Remember that in their own way they do care

    I know it's really hard when you are frustrated but try to avoid apportioning blame. Keep in your head that the teacher is probably as lost and frustrated as you are - even if they are unable to admit it. I know it seems obvious to those of us who live with Autism day in day out what should be done, but the reality is most people don't live in our world and don't understand. We can teach them, but it does take time.

- Think about your negotiation skills

    And last but not least, my top tip is to pretend you are negotiating with your child. You are all expert negotiators, if you weren't you wouldn't get through each day. Apply the skills you have learnt to working with teachers and before you know it they will be on side.

Strategies

Understanding Triggers And Why They Matter

It's likely that at some point along the line you will want to sit and think about why your child is reacting in the way they are to certain situations. For some children that could be because they are displaying behaviours that challenge those around them, for others it could be that they are struggling to concentrate at certain times of the day, or that their anxiety levels are preventing them from doing things that you know that they would enjoy doing.

Understanding their triggers - the little things that contribute to them behaving and feeing a certain way can be a really important part of this process.

I believe firmly that all behaviour - good or bad - happens for a reason. And it's much easier for us to understand and develop that behaviour if we know why a child is doing it. Without knowing the cause it's much harder to make changes.

The reality is that a child's reactions don't occur in isolation, and if something isn't quite working one or more of the following factors are usually involved:

- Anxiety
- Sensory overwhelm
- Unexpected change
- Low self esteem
- A desire mask true thoughts and feelings
- Demand avoidance
- Task avoidance
- Fear of failure
- Attempting to fit in with a peer group without understanding the rules

In order to begin to help our children tackle the behaviour (whether that is behaviour that challenges us in the conventional sense, or a reaction such as withdrawal that we are not sure how to handle) we need to understand the root cause.

For some children and young people this will be obvious as the reaction will occur simultaneously or immediately after the trigger. Whereas for others it will be more complex to work out, either because they mask their true feelings until they feel like they are in a safe place, or because the behaviour is a result of several small triggers building up throughout the day.

The types of triggers

Let's start with anxiety:

Gaining a full understanding of your child's anxieties is a big step in being able to reduce them and indeed to helping your child understand them. Fully understanding why someone feels (and therefore acts) the way that they do also helps us be more tempered in our reaction and therefore ensures that inadvertently we don't add to the anxiety.

There are several ways you can approach this subject with your child:

- ✓ Ask them to make a list of all of the things that worry them or make them feel anxious.
- ✓ Sit and talk to your child about any worries that they might have.
- ✓ Take a more structured approach by using one of the outlines which you can access via the link on page 146.

If your child is unable or unwilling to discuss this with you, try to get as many of the adults involved in their life as possible to make a list of the things that they feel provoke feelings of anxiety. If you decide to adopt this method it's crucial to bring together people from different areas of the child's life. At the bare minimum a member of school staff and you as parents should contribute to the anxiety analysis. Once you have this data it will make it much easier for you to tackle those areas that your child finds hard.

Once you've established the causes of anxiety, it's then time to start working on any other triggers. It's likely that you'll already be aware of the larger more instant ones but what you want to try to do now is to identify those smaller triggers that build up throughout the day.

Sensory sensitivities are a good next step to tackle:

- ✓ Talk to your child and observe them carefully in different environments.
- ✓ Do they struggle to process your voice when it's noisy?
- ✓ Or perhaps they shut down when you go into the supermarket?
- ✓ Take a look at our sensory sensitivities checklist (See page 146 for the link) and try to identify which of those things your child finds difficult.
- ✓ Where possible ask your child for their input. Asking an open question is the best way to do it e.g. 'Do you prefer being in the room when the lights are on or off?' or 'Do you like it outside when it is windy or do you prefer it when there is no breeze?' Some children and young people will be able to explain to you why they prefer one over the other, others won't yet be able to verbalise why but will have a distinct preference.

Next, you will want to determine the extent to which *unexpected changes, low self esteem, masking, demand avoidance, task avoidance* and *fear of failure* are coming into play.

Often these are difficult to analyse as individual features and the best way to discover which of these triggers is having an impact and the extent to which they are having an impact is best identified via the use of daily tracking. Using either the adult led, child led, or a combination of both types of tracking sheets (see page 146 for the link) can help you identify patterns over a period of time. So for instance over a period of several weeks, you can identify that problems occur later in the day because of the unexpected change of a wet playtime, or that problems always occur when written work is presented as students become anxious about making mistakes.

To get as accurate a picture as possible it is important that the tracking is done across settings. In the case of children that mask, the difference in their responses at home and at school may be significant.

Reducing Environmental Triggers

Busy and unpredictable places can be extremely challenging for children on the Spectrum. Therefore creating a home environment where they can escape from the challenges of the real world is often a big step towards reducing Meltdowns.

So what can you do that will make a difference:

→ **The home in general**

Order throughout the house is important. Although your child may not be tidy (neither of mine are), that doesn't mean that they won't benefit from an ordered environment. Making sure that things within the house have places that aren't deviated from, will help them to relax within their environment.

Ensure that there is always an escape route both from you and from siblings. When put under pressure children with Autism tend to demonstrate what is called a 'fight or flight response.' You are much more likely to escape the fight response if there is a way of your child taking some time away to regulate their emotions before returning to the family group.

If lots of visitors (or indeed any visitors) arrive, ensure your child understands that they don't need to stay in the main areas, they can escape to their room whenever they need to.

Try to avoid letting your child claim communal spaces as theirs. Whilst it often appears easier initially to move the rest of the family and therefore avoid confrontation, it is a pattern that can be hard to break. Keep in mind the fact that routine is important to children on the Spectrum and that if you allow this once they will expect it again. It's a pattern that if established will make it increasingly difficult to invite visitors and will breed resentment among siblings.

Your child should be encouraged to see their bedroom as their sanctuary and a place to escape to when needed.

→ **Your child's bedroom**

Having somewhere to call their own is very important for children on the Spectrum. Whilst it's totally understandable that they may need (or even prefer in some cases) to share a bedroom with siblings, it is critical that within that room they have a space that is dedicated to them.

Creating well thought out storage where items can be safely put away to avoid breakages in times of crisis, and to prevent anxiety that new items will change the look of the room can be a huge help.

Having a space to crawl into if they are feeling overwhelmed can also prove a useful tool. For younger children a den or tent of some kind is often a preferred option, whereas for teenagers a cosy bed surrounded by their own things proves a good choice. If space is of the essence consider the type of tent that goes over the bed itself, giving them their own space, without sacrificing space to play. Cushions, a throw or weighted blankets can help those who benefit from deep pressure.

A bedroom should be a place of relaxation and yet somewhere your child is willing to go to calm down if they are becoming anxious or distressed.

A selection of products that are easily available to use when anxious are helpful to keep out at all times. Depending on the young person in question this could include a favourite book, a photo book containing pictures of things they have enjoyed, music to listen to, objects related to their special interest or sensory items to fiddle with.

Technology can be a particularly difficult decision. Many young people on the Spectrum use their technology as a way of communicating with others - something that we as parents want to promote. They also often use it as a way to decompress, especially after a busy day at school surrounded by people. Again this is positive usage which serves an important purpose. However, if that technology is left in the room overnight it can cause problems - especially because many young people with Autism struggle to sleep. Starting an early habit of bringing technology downstairs at bed time can help, especially if it's exchanged for hot chocolate and a preferred bed time snack. This can also make leaving the room and getting ready for school in the morning a less stressful experience for parents.

→ **Out and about**

Leaving the house is very difficult for many children and young people with Autism but there are things you can do to help to reduce Meltdowns when you are out.

Shopping can be particularly problematic, especially on a busy Saturday afternoon. It's a non-preferred activity which is high stress. Shopping at a time when stores are likely to be quiet or shopping online are both preferred alternatives. Many children and young people will cope for short periods of time, but an extended trip is always high risk. If this is something your child finds difficult and that you want to work on, building trips up slowly is a good way to start, slowly extending the amount of shops you visit and the time you spend in them.

Ensure that you agree on a signal or word to use before leaving the house so that your child can tell you when things are getting too much. Building in breaks in quieter and/ or preferred places will help them to cope for longer.

Taking a camera for your chid to use to document their day can be helpful, especially when visiting new places. Viewing the world through a camera lens feels less daunting than viewing it in real life, it also provides a much needed role and function for the young person to accomplish.

The App Pokemon Go has been found to be similarly helpful for some families, bringing a young person's special interest into a trip can help them to cope with the challenge of the environmental factors around as they are concentrating on catching or evolving the Pokemon in their care.

The real key is to remember that helping your child cope with the world around them is also about understanding (and emphasising to others) that there are things we, as adults, can do that will make coping that little bit easier. Thinking about the environment that they are in is often the first step in achieving that.

Tackling Task Based Triggers

Starting a new task is something that so many of our young people find hard. Even if it's something that they really want to do, taking that first step to start can be incredibly difficult. This chapter focuses on ways that you can reduce the number of Meltdowns and anxiety surrounding tasks.

How to reduce Meltdowns and anxiety:

→ **Transitions between one task and another**

Transitions are often difficult for children on the Spectrum. Using a timer or verbally counting down until a new task begins can help prepare young people for the change coming.

Visual clues, such as visual timetables (pictorial or written), now and next boards or traffic light systems can help children and young people to see not only when to expect a transition, but also what will happen afterwards.

For some children handing them an object related to the task they need to do wherever they are will help them to make that transition. E.g. handing them a spoon in the living room can be a good cue to go to the table.

Children and young people will have particular difficulty transitioning if they have not completed the original task. Where possible finishing the original task before asking them to move on is likely to result in a better outcome. (I do know in real life sometimes this just isn't possible.)

→ **Task overwhelm**

Looking at a new task can often feel overwhelming, children and young people with Autism often find the thought of beginning something new difficult, because they are unsure where to start. Breaking that task down can go a long way to help.

Post-it notes are literally my favourite thing in the whole world!

They are easily available, cheap to buy and come in their 100s. They are also incredible at using to break tasks down. Depending on the task and the person attempting the task, you can either give them several Post-it notes complete with the break down right at the beginning, or sit down and work out the steps together. Once the step is complete they can bin the note. This can work for anything from tidying their bedroom, to making a sandwich, to completing a homework task. The humble Post-it note is as versatile as you want to make it.

Tick lists are popular with some children and young people as not only do they help break a task down (again this can either be made before the task starts or done collaboratively with your child) but they also help to give a sense of accomplishment as each item is completed.

→ **A lack of understanding about the reason for needing to do the task**

One of the areas that many people with Autism struggle with is central coherence. This means that although they can often see small details very clearly it can be hard for them to understand the full picture. Explaining why what you are asking is important can thus make a huge difference to a young person's willingness to do that task. It's important to remember that what seems obvious to you doesn't necessarily appear obvious to a young person with Autism. Talking through the need to do a task e.g. take a shower often helps them to understand why you nag so much about the task being completed. Which in turn makes the pressure to complete the task less frustrating.

→ **Fear of making a mistake during the task**

Many children and young people on the Spectrum struggle with the idea of getting things wrong. They are specialists and perfectionists - preferring to be experts in a select number of things rather than generalists who happily throw themselves into things without knowing if they'll succeed.

If it's a new task, start with just one element at a time. E.g. if teeth brushing is something that just isn't happening, for the first week the only part of the task is taking the toothbrush out of the jar. Week two is holding the toothbrush in one hand and the toothpaste in the other and week three is putting the toothpaste on the brush. By the time week four rolls around putting the brush in their mouth feels a lot scary than they expected and when they need to start actively using it in week six the fear has often evaporated.

Tell them your expectations. Say it's ok if it goes wrong because no-one needs to see it, or tell them that you always get this wrong too. Make sure that they know you will be proud of them for trying rather than accomplishing the task.

The key here is to remember that often when a child refuses to do something there is more to the 'no' than often meets the eye. Once you understand the reason behind the answer, it's much easier to tackle that 'no' and turn it into a 'yes.' On the whole, children and young people want to please us and if we think carefully about how we set up the tasks we give them, we can help them to do just that.

Preventing Sensory Overload

One of the things that can cause significant amounts of distress to children and young people with Autism are sensory triggers. Ironically despite this they can be some of the most difficult triggers to identify. This is because unlike for example an unexpected change which often provokes an instant response, sensory overload can build gradually throughout the day. This means that something which seemingly has no effect on a child in the early part of the day could provoke a much bigger reaction later on.

These suggestions are aimed at helping you to develop strategies to prevent the build up that can occur from sensory sensitivities. Not all of the issues mentioned here will be appropriate to your family, but if you complete the sensory profile which you can access via the link on page 146, it will give you a good indication of which may be useful to try.

Sensory sensitivities

→ **Light**

Experiment with different lighting in your home, especially in areas where your child spends a lot of their time. Bulbs with smaller wattages or lamps with a tint of colour can both make a big difference to a young person's ability to cope.

Consider having blinds put up at your child's window which allow them to control the amount of daylight which enters the room.

If light is a big factor for your child it may be worth considering an Irlen Assessment, although the glasses are quite expensive the overlays are very affordable and can make a big difference to a young person's willingness to carry out tasks in brighter areas. (N.B. I have no affiliation with Irlen, nor do I have any professional experience of their services. I have however had personal experience of their products and seen a big difference for some young people after they have begun to use them.)

→ **Sound**

Experiment with different ways of enabling your child to block out noises they find difficult. Ear defenders or ear plugs work well for some children and young people, others prefer to wear headphones playing their favourite music. One louder more consistent noise is often easier for children to cope with than multiple different noises coming from multiple different directions.

Provide opportunities for your child to spend time somewhere quiet to recharge their batteries; this may involve having access to a different room at a family party or taking regular sensory breaks in the car on family days out.

→ **Smell**

Be aware that smells are often significantly stronger for children on the Spectrum than they seem to us. Thinking about your route when you are out can be particularly important, places like the perfume department or fish market can be particularly challenging. If you need to go through them, preparing your child before you enter for the strong smells they will experience can be helpful.

Young people with Autism can find changes to shower gel, shampoo and washing powder particularly challenging as they are hyper aware of how those products normally smell. If you need to change the product, or your normal product is out of stock try to involve your child in the decision about which product to switch to in order to try to find one which they don't find too overwhelming.

→ **Taste**

As parents at home we are often skilled in creating our child's favourite meals, when we are out and about things can be a little more challenging. Ensuring others your children spend time with are warned about their food needs, and that alternatives are available if they are to eat in other places can go a long way to avoiding Meltdowns.

Practicing with them things they can say and giving them scripts they can follow if a meal they are served isn't something that they feel they can eat can also go a really long way to giving them the confidence to eat out of the house.

→ **Touch**

Often people see touch just as a problem with others touching the child. In actual fact this is often a vast over simplification. Children who struggle with touch often also struggle with other sensations on their skin. This can mean that wind, drafts and other sensations can also make them feel overwhelmed.

Clothing can also be an issue, with children finding some textures very challenging. Over the years we have found online shopping works best for us, it means that any item can be tried on several times over a period of 48 hours to ensure that it's going to be comfortable enough to wear. It has also stopped numerous arguments (mainly initiated by me) about clothes that have been bought never being worn.

If seams are a problem, seamless socks and underwear can be found via a quick online search and can prove a huge help to some families.

For those children who find breezes and drafts difficult, roller blinds can prove a good alternative to curtains as these can be rolled fully upwards and therefore flap less if a small breeze occurs.

Sensory sensitivities are one of the most unrecognised difficulties that children on the Spectrum face, and few realise the impact they can have on every aspect of their life. By putting into practice the strategies above that are relevant for your child you will start to see an increasing degree of willingness to participate in things they have previously found overwhelming - making life easier not only for your child but for the whole family.

Raising Self Esteem Whilst Reducing The Fear Of Making Mistakes

A lack of self-esteem is very common in children and young people with Autism. It can feel hard to fit into the world when you are different, especially as a teenager when conformity never seems more important.

Showing young people that difference is a good thing, and that they are both valuable and important as a person is crucial.

The following activities can help:

→ **Find things they excel at and promote them.**

All too often we focus on the things our children can't do or struggle with and spend our time practicing them. Instead stop for a while and allow your child to do whatever it is they are good at, give them a chance to experience success and being the best.

→ **Introduce them to good examples**

Research what other adults with Autism have achieved, where possible, relate it to activities that will interest your child (a quick Google will reveal a wealth of information, but if you need any additional help please do join our free Facebook Community and ask).

→ **Find ways for them to help others.**

There is nothing quite like the feeling of helping someone else to show you how worthwhile you are. For older children, why not ask if there is a way they would be able to help younger children at school, maybe by listening to them read or by teaching them how to do a simple skill.

→ **Celebrate the positives**

Buy a notebook and turn it into a Happy Book, that way they can write down the things that have gone right at the end of each day. This can then be referred back to on days where your child feels like there is nothing that they can do right.

Keep a record of all achievements, however small and either keep small memories of them in a box (e.g. a serviette from a time they tried a new food at a restaurant) or write them down in a book. That way when they are worried about whether they have the ability to try something new you already have a huge wealth of evidence to show them that they can.

Making mistakes

Making mistakes is incredibly difficult for many children and young people with Autism. And often the fear of getting something wrong can make doing something they find difficult or new extremely challenging. As children get older, this is one fear that gets particularly hard to admit, especially if they are around their peers. Instead young people can act out, become aggressive or withdraw out of an inability to act and a fear of looking stupid.

So how can we help them to see that sometimes mistakes are an essential part of life:

- ✓ Model making your own mistakes, as well as both correcting and/ or moving on from them.
- ✓ Talk about the fact that sometimes mistakes can be a very good thing. A quick Google will show you a whole host of inventions that came about entirely because mistakes happened.
- ✓ Tell them that you are proud of them when they make a mistake and yet still carry on. That their mistakes make their achievements more worthwhile not less worthwhile.
- ✓ Talk about some of the worst mistakes you have made and how things have turned out ok in the end.
- ✓ Provide constant reassurance that it is ok to get things wrong and to make mistakes.

✓ Ask what would make making a mistake easier, some children and young people prefer for instance to write in a pencil rather than pen because mistakes are easier to rectify.

All too often the system focuses on what our children can't do. From lists of their struggles given at diagnosis, to standardised tests that often aren't quite the right fit. As parents therefore, it's our job to show them just how incredible they are. And that can start *right now*. Why not stop reading for a moment and write your child a note telling them just how incredible they are - I promise you it will be well worth the effort.

The Power Of Special Interests

Special interests are often underestimated in terms of their value, both by teachers and parents. The reality is though that if we properly harness their potential, they can be a valuable tool in making our children feel more relaxed in both helping them find the things that challenge them easier and promoting learning.

Research shows that children with Autism process their feelings about their special interest in the same place in their brain that those who are neurotypical reserve for those who they love. The feelings that spending time exploring it provoke are therefore incredibly powerful and should not be underestimated.

Special interests can be incorporated into most parts of family life with a bit of creativity.

The following are some suggestions to get you going:

→ **Emotional regulation**

Never are special interests more important than when trying to help a child or young person to regulate their emotions.

The key is that the activity chosen should be something that will calm rather than overstimulate them, and something that will not be too difficult to move on from afterwards - especially if the reason for their disregulation is task related and you need to get them back on track.

Activities that work well are:

- Having a conversation with a trusted adult about an element of their special interest.
- Organising and discussing a special interest related event for later in the day.
- Reading a chapter of a book about their special interest (depending on the length of the chapter).

- Watching an episode related to their special interest (depending on the length of the episode).
- Ordering a set of objects related to their special interest (this could be organising their You-Gi-Oh cards ready for a later game, or lining up a set of special interest related objects).

The key is that the activity should be one which eliminates any chance of frustration as your child's emotions are already heightened. So playing a video game, challenging a friend to a game of You-Gi-Oh, or opening a blind bag to see if its contents are the desired one, whilst special interest related would not be advised at this particular time.

→ **Reward schemes**

Incorporating special interests into your reward schemes will set them quite literally on fire. Knowing what will excite your children is key, but easy inexpensive choices which have gone down well with others are singular Yu-Gi-Oh, Pokemon and Match Attack Cards, earning time to watch a favourite film and time spent with a family member watching YouTube videos whilst discussing their merits.

→ **During free time**

Do not underestimate how much your children will enjoy spending time sitting chatting about their special interest either with you or with a friend who has a similar interest. Free time is something that lots of young people on the Spectrum find difficult, especially if they are away from home, as it's when their social and communication difficulties are most challenged. For some, especially younger children, a box full of tangible items related to their special interest will prove a valuable tool especially for taking with you on days out or for using during break times at school.

→ **As distraction**

I'm a big believer in averting a crisis whenever possible. Whether it's a piece of homework that your child looks at and decides is too challenging, an argument with a friend or a confrontation about a rule, distraction is my method of choice. A quick conversation about a special interest often reminds them that you are human and therefore technically at least might be being reasonable. It's therefore much easier to then gently persuade them to return back to the task in hand. The direct method isn't always the most effective.

→ **For building relationships**

If there are family members or friends that your child struggles to relate to, utilising their special interest can be a great way to build bridges. I have learnt over the years that if I want my students to listen to what I need them to learn I have to be prepared to be interested in the things that are important to them. I have learnt a lot over the years about all manner of topics I may never have known anything about otherwise. But more important than any fact that I have learnt is that for a while I am able to enter a world which is important to my students, to see their eyes light up, and to meet them on their playing field. It's during this time that we as adults can truly build a relationship with them, in order to enable us to have the best possible relationship.

→ **For tackling homework**

We all know that homework can be a battle, but with a little creativity and willingness from the teacher to adapt and/ or let you adapt the task special interests can really help children to buy into the task. It is surprisingly easy to relate academic tasks to so many of our children's special interests. From comprehension lessons based on Pokemon, discussions about habitats related to Minecraft or looking at the conventions of Fairytales through Disney characters. If you know your child and their interest well enough, there is very little you cannot relate to it. It will take a little more time, but trust me once you have seen just how much they enjoy it you'll never go back to doing things any other way.

If there is one phrase I want you to remember from this book it's, *'If you want a child to come into your world, sometimes you have to meet them half way'*. Their special interests are the best possible way of doing exactly this.

Reducing Demands Without Lowering Expectations

In Autism circles, reducing demands is often seen as a strategy for those young people with Pathological Demand Avoidance (a specific branch of the Spectrum).

But the real reality is that many children and young people both on and off the Spectrum respond well to PDA strategies. I tell teachers at work that, *'Good Autism teaching is good everyone teaching'* and never has that been more true than when it comes to the strategies used with young people with Pathological Demand Avoidance.

If your child becomes anxious when they are not in control of a situation, struggles with authority or feels backed into a corner when a task is assigned it's likely that these strategies will be particularly useful for them. As many authorities currently do not officially diagnose or recognise PDA, it's likely that many children are undiagnosed. Trying these strategies won't hurt and might make a huge difference.

So what exactly is PDA or Pathological Demand Avoidance?

Pathological Demand Avoidance or PDA as it's often known comes under the Autism umbrella. But children or young people who have PDA often have a distinct profile. Like others with an Autism diagnosis they will experience difficulties with social communication and interaction, and display behaviours, activities and interests which are repetitive and restricted. However, those with PDA will also exhibit a pronounced need to be in control.

Their need for this control is anxiety driven and leads to a need to avoid the demands and expectations of others. Although children and young people who have PDA often present with behaviours that look as though they are being caused by anger and/ or wilful disobedience, behaviours are much more likely to be caused by fear, anxiety and confusion. This last point should be remembered and at the forefront of any strategies used.

Many authorities in the UK do not recognise PDA as a distinct condition which needs its own diagnostic criteria. Autism is a Spectrum and as Demand Avoidance is included in the NICE criteria for Autism diagnosis, many areas do not feel a separate diagnosis is necessary. Despite this professionals working with children with Autism are increasingly aware of the condition and of the need to use distinct strategies to ensure young people reach their potential.

Reducing demands is therefore key to success:

If your child has PDA reducing the demands you give them will decrease their anxiety levels and therefore reduce the amount of challenging behaviours that you see. This doesn't mean that you need to, or even should lower your expectations.

Instead you just need approach things in a different way:

→ **Choose your language carefully**

As both a mum and a teacher I'm always conscious that I often feel more of a demand machine than a person. Unless I think about it consciously sometimes I can give as many as six demands a minute 'Come in, put your coat away, put your bag in the cupboard, no don't run into your brother, make sure you turn the light of when you finish in the bathroom....' and the list goes on. The reality is nobody likes being bossed about and I'm pretty sure that my daughter actually knows all of these things, they are part of her daily routine.. yet unless I'm careful and check myself they pop out of my mouth without thinking about it.

→ **Consider Using The Written Word To Your Advantage**

Written schedules can feel less threatening than verbal ones.. after all the piece of paper isn't going to argue back with you. For daily routines checklists of this kind can give your child independence and stop you needing to make demands as frequently.

If you and your child disagree abut something, arguments are easy to get into - words fly around without thinking about it and before we know it more demands are coming out of our mouths, which only serve to inflame an already difficult situation. Writing down the argument allows both parties to have their say, to feel heard and to reflect before committing words to paper. I work it like a verbal conversation, so to begin with I would write a question on a piece of paper and hand it over. A good way to start is, 'I'm sorry that I've upset you, would you like to tell me how I can help.' You aren't saying you have done anything wrong but you are acknowledging that your decision has caused upset and that you want to help. This in itself often goes a long way to defuse a situation. From this point you pass the paper back and forth both writing your answers in turn until a mutual resolution has been agreed upon.

→ **Model rather than tell**

Statistics tell us that young people learn far more by watching and doing than they do by being told. So for some things it's much easier just to keep demonstrating... eventually it will rub off. Say please and thank you (excessively if needed) especially to your child, sit at the table the way you want them to sit and make sure you have a tidy room if you expect them to. Gradually you will begin to see that your child follows suit, the things that you want them to do become the done thing, the usual thing, rather than the demanded thing. The key is that although this approach will take time to work, both you and your child will feel less frustrated, which will ultimately improve anxiety levels, and strengthen your relationship. You will stop feeling as though your requests (demands in your child's eyes) are being ignored and they will stop feeling as though too many demands are being made on them and thus feel more in control and therefore able to comply.

→ **Always give a way out**

Simple non-confrontational choices can be a great way of avoiding giving demands: 'We need some milk for breakfast, do you think we should go to the supermarket or the corner shop?', I need to hoover your room tomorrow, do you want to move things to one side first so you know where they are and can put them back as you like them, or would you like me to do it?' As parents there will always be unwanted things that we have to do. In the first example had you told your child you were going to the corner shop they would have been annoyed at the demand, by giving them the choice they are able to choose the least painful of the two choices and feel more in control about what is happening.

Give them somewhere to escape if things get too much. If you're at home this could be the use of their bedroom, or the use of a dark den or tent if they share a room. If you're out and about, finding open space nearby or having access to the car if needed can provide a space to escape from the wider world if needed.

Lastly ensure that they have a way of letting you easily know when things have got too much, even though the words can't be found. This could be in the form of a token to hand over, a time out card, or a code word. When we use code words we tend to pick something silly like 'Orange' or 'Pear'. It means that others have no idea what's happening and adds a little bit of humour to relax everyone into the mix.

→ **Make sure they see you, the person, rather than you the demand machine**

As with other children on the Spectrum, special interests are a powerful tool. If you (which as a parent you often need to) are giving lots of demands try to take time out of each day to connect with your child via their special interest. This could be as simple as showing an interest in what they have built in Minecraft that day, or asking them which You-Gi-Oh cards they are on the hunt for at the moment. It doesn't need to be an extended activity, just something to remind them that you care about the things that they care about.

→ **Use humour (carefully)**

The reality with humour is that it can be an amazing tool, or an absolute disaster. It rarely falls in the middle. It's therefore one that needs to be carefully judged.

For me humour tends to work best when it relates to an 'in joke' something that becomes a way of breaking tension between me and the young person involved. With one student I worked with, all I needed to do was mention the name of a park I knew he loved and he would burst out laughing, another constantly used to tease me about my love of all things Disney - I knew therefore that mentioning Disney if he was starting to get stressed or anxious would deflect his mood and he would resume the teasing, and therefore often do what was being asked of him.

Testing humour out when not using it alongside demands is essential. Only if you are sure it's a topic that your child will find funny should it be used at more challenging times.

The key to remember is, the reduction of demands is often about *phraseology and method* rather than changing what actually needs to be done. *It's about being creative and trying new things.* And most of all it's about approaching everything as flexibly as you can.

Using Schedules To Reduce Meltdowns

Having spent most of my teaching career working with children who have behavioural difficulties caused by their anxieties, and the last eleven years parenting my daughter, schedules have become one of my most used tools in reducing the number of Meltdowns that occur; both in my classroom and in my home.

What is a schedule?

A schedule is a list, which can be either written, pictorial or both, which provides a child with a structure either within an activity or for their whole day.

Does a schedule need to stay fixed throughout the day?

Absolutely not. The beauty of schedules is a change in your day is much less likely to cause upset because a child can immediately see that although one activity has changed the rest of their day remains the same. Without a schedule, children who struggle with change, often panic even if a small change is made to their day. Their immediate assumption is that if one change is made, the rest of their day is in jeopardy. This can mean that often a very small change can spark a Meltdown, whereas if the change is visually seen on the schedule with the remaining events staying the same, their reactions are often more in proportion.

Why are schedules helpful?

Schedules help make life more predictable and when life is more predictable, children are often calmer. When they're feeling calmer, they are less likely to overreact to other situations, which makes Meltdowns less likely.

Is a written or pictorial schedule best?

Only you can decide that, there is no right or wrong answer. To a large extent it will depend on which medium you feel your child will respond best to, and which you think they will be most comfortable using.

Can children help to make schedules?

Absolutely, schedules can be as professional or as homemade as you want to make them. They can take the form of a list on an electronic device, or be handwritten on a piece of paper. There are no hard and fast rules about how they should look.

Are there any other rules?

Just one. Whatever is written on the schedule must be followed. Changes can be made, as has been discussed, but they must be made on the schedule as well as in life so that children can see visually what is happening?

Will this work for all children?

No, I'm a firm believer in the fact that nothing works for everyone. However, it's another tool to add to your armoury, something else to try out. Who knows, you might just find it makes a difference.

Getting Out Of The House Without A Meltdown

One of the most common things I hear from parents of children with Autism is that the morning routine is their most stressful time of the day. The combination of anxiety and a lack of naturally produced Melatonin means that achieving and staying asleep is often challenging, so when morning rolls round the whole family is often far from rested. Add to that an uncertain school day ahead, family hustle and bustle, and pressure to get out of the house on time and it really is the perfect recipe for a Meltdown. It therefore isn't a surprise that it is so often a challenging time.

In our house there are a number of things which help us to co-exist in the mornings without too many raging arguments and/ or tears. I'm not saying they are a magic wand, we still have our bad days. But life is definitely easier than it was before we introduced them.

Morning routine tips:

→ **Most important is the schedule**

My daughter hates to be nagged (don't we all), and I am definitely a nagger by nature (just ask the Other Half)! Having a written schedule of things that need to be done which can be ticked off as she goes along means that I can keep track of how near we are to leaving the door and she can have her independence. We use schedules for lots of different things in our house and always have, but none have made more difference than this one. Whether you decide to use photographs, images or a written list, the key is to emphasise what makes your child independent so they feel more in control of their morning.

→ **Build in free time, especially if your child gets anxious about being late**

The more time we have the less likely anyone will get anxious about being late. This means that we all feel calmer as we get ready. And if things do go wrong lateness doesn't add to an already stressful situation. On an average morning we are all ready at least twenty minutes before we leave. We also arrive at school and sing Disney songs ten minutes before the gates open. As we live close by, this means that if something has been forgotten we have time to turn back home and retrieve it without being late.

→ **Don't underestimate the importance of a reward**

There are some mornings that I know are going to be difficult. In our house this includes the first day of a new term, swimming days, and days where something unusual and non-preferred is planned. On those days I try to build in rewards to help things go a little more smoothly. Whether it's a nice breakfast to set the day off on a good footing or the promise of a trip to the park after school. Something nice to combat the evil of the day usually goes down well.

What if none of that works?

The truth is that for some children, however perfect your morning routine is, their anxiety will still prevail. There are however other things you can do to help reduce their anxiety to enable them to leave the house:

→ **Create an anxiety profile:**

Discuss with your child exactly what it is that is making them anxious and together work on strategies to combat those anxieties. If it's worry about the place you are going rather than leaving the house itself that is the problem, strategies may also need to be put into place at school.

→ **Keep calm**

Easier said than done I know! I am far better at it as a teacher than I am as a mum. Remember that Rome wasn't built in a day, and that you almost certainly aren't doing anything wrong. Sometimes even despite our best efforts things don't happen overnight. Take small steps, whether that's doing the journey to school but agreeing not to go through the door, or going into school for one lesson at a time. Once small steps have been achieved you can then move onto larger ones.

→ **Talk to others**

Sometimes it's really hard to look at your own life and be objective... I know I've been there. If there are professionals that you can access to help you come up with new strategies, it's worth giving them a try. Whether it's your child's teacher, a psychologist or your local Autism team, they may just have a strategy that you haven't tried yet. It's hard to have professionals in your home, I know, we've been there. But sometimes from the outside it's just easier to see things that we miss when we are close to them.

If you don't have access to professionals who can help, parent support groups can be a fantastic resource, whether in person or online. Not only are other parents great at sharing ideas but they are fantastic at making you feel less alone.

→ **Is PDA in the mix?**

If your child has Pathological Demand Avoidance mornings may well be particularly challenging. Not only are they filled with demands from you (Get out of bed, Get dressed. Eat your breakfast etc..), they know that a day full of demands at school will follow. Try as much as possible to reduce the demands you are giving. Think carefully about how you phrase your requests and be prepared to compromise.

Remember, arriving late to school is better than not getting there at all; take your time, stay calm and above all *be kind to yourself.* You are doing a great job.

Teaching Friendship Skills

In those early days right after diagnosis, my predominant worry was what if my daughter never made any friends. What if she spent her days alone.

I spent the next five years matchmaking. I organised play dates which went wrong (sometimes disastrously so), moved to an estate with lots of children (which lasted less than a year before we resumed countryside living), and signed her up for every extra curricular club going. And then I stood back. She was anxious. I was anxious. What I was doing clearly wasn't working.

It did however teach me a valuable lesson, and one that I've carried over into my professional life as well.

I realised that I can give my daughter and my students friendship skills. I can teach them the strategies they need to be successful in relationships, but I cannot control their friendships.

They have to be allowed to do that themselves.

My top tips for teaching friendship skills are:

- ✓ **Teach the basics**

    It's important to remember that even the most academically able child or young person is likely to struggle with the social nuances of friendships. Add to that the anxiety of doing something you know you struggle with and a hatred of making mistakes and it's easy to see why youngsters on the Spectrum find friendships challenging.

    I believe in teaching and practicing the basics, from how to ask someone to play, to how to change the game to something children are happier playing in role play format, to how to put things right after an argument. Spending time each week practicing these skills, with you playing one role and your child playing another can make a big difference. Make sure that you make some mistakes, your children will love correcting you when you get it wrong. The key is to gradually add in new scripts each week until your child feels confident with them. Giving them a chance to learn new ones at a time when their emotions aren't charged so that they feel more empowered when they are in real life situations.

✓ **Allow for down time**

Both at home and at school it is important not to insist that children are constantly social during their free time. The school day is hard for many children on the Spectrum. They spend it engaging in activities they don't want to do, listening to staff they don't want to listen to and working with other students they don't want to work with. So whilst I believe in giving opportunities to access social activities, I don't believe in making it compulsory. If a child wants to sit and read a book, go on a computer or just to spend some time alone, that is ok too. Spending free time alone doing their own thing, can recharge a child's batteries ready for the day ahead. I do not believe in imposing friendships.

✓ **Try to find other young people who share your child's special interests.**

There is nothing that excites me more than the referral paperwork for a new student that has the same interest as one of my existing students. I know that my students have a better chance of developing a connection with each other if they have a strong shared interest. I've long since realised that actual matchmaking doesn't work. But if I construct activities based on the joint interest, I know that the students will naturally gravitate together.

So whether you are trying to encourage friendships with others at school, or with young people out of school this is usually a good place to start. It makes friendship significantly less stressful if you know that the person you are talking to enjoys discussing the same things that you do.

✓ **Speak to school about support during free time**

All too often support is left in place for lesson time, then withdrawn during free time. Whereas in actual fact for most children on the Spectrum, free time is the time they need that support the most. Even if your child has 1:1 support, their teaching assistant is entitled to a break during the day and this is often timed to coincide with the break time of the children. Talking to the school about whether they feel they could adjust the role of support staff so they can be around to facilitate during these times, is often a good first step in teaching friendship skills. By monitoring friendships from a slight distance, it's easy to pull a child quickly aside to advise them on how to solve an issue before it becomes a problem. Ensuring that friendships are maintained for longer, children feel successful in their relationships and that they learn the skills needed for the future.

In summary, the *real key* is to give your children the skills they need to develop friendships. But remember, ultimately, the choice of whether to play alone or with others is *their right* and *their choice*.

Structuring A New Activity

For many young people with Autism starting a new activity or going somewhere new can be really challenging. For some difficulties with doing this can lead to a life that consists of only home and school with little in the middle.

Whilst this isn't necessarily a bad thing, especially for younger children who are often exhausted after the pressures of the school day and need the downtime that home provides. Older children often get to the point where they would like to take part in other activities but become overwhelmingly anxious about doing so.

This chapter aims to give a step by step approach to thinking about and introducing a new activity.

Structuring new activities

Think carefully about the activity choice

Choosing an activity your child is likely to get intrinsic enjoyment from, and if possible one that is related to their special interest is most likely to achieve a favourable outcome. Talk to them about the kind of activities they might like to try out, and let them know that it's ok to try a few before finding one that's the right fit for them.

Consider the environment

Taking a look at the alternative venues that the activity is held in and their suitability for your child is key. Do they prefer to be indoors or outdoors? Do they cope better in a large room with plenty of space or in a smaller venue that's more contained? If they like you to be around is there somewhere you will be able to sit nearby?

Talk to the teacher/ instructor/ group leader

Getting a feel for the person in charge of the activity will help you to gauge how well they will relate to your child, and how well your child will relate to them. Don't be afraid to ask if they have Autism experience and whether they would be happy to listen to the strategies you give them. Activities can be a great way of building self esteem, but sadly feeling as though they have failed at them can act in reverse. Getting the right group leader can make a huge difference to the potential for success.

Go for a pre-visit

Visiting the building, watching the activity for a short time or meeting the teacher prior to attending the group/ activity for the first time can make a big difference. Knowing that you will be with them for the whole time, that they will only be staying for a very limited time and that they can leave at any point they need to can all be key to ensuring those who find new things difficult, feel confident to step through the door.

Arrange a taster session

I have lost count of the number of activities that we have been to over the years only to never return again. Activities that all too often we have signed up for and paid for a term in advance. Most groups though, if you ask will offer a taster session prior to asking you to sign up. This session will give both you and your child chance to assess whether this activity is the right one for them, rather than having the pressure of feeling like you have to make it work.

Find a friend

If a friend – or at least a familiar face – happens to be in the room new activities tend to be easier. It can be hard walking into a sea of unfamiliar faces. So doing your research in advance and trying to find people within the group your child will recognise can be really helpful. If you know their parents, arranging for them to meet you outside so that your children can walk through the door together can make a huge difference.

Negotiate the terms

Talk to your child in advance about what would make the activity easier for them. Do they want you to stay with them? Do they need a calm day before or a list of exactly what will be happening during the session?

Keep it pressure free

It is really important especially in the early days of a new activity to take as much pressure off both you and your child's shoulders as possible. For some children and young people this may involve building the time spent at the activity up gradually week by week, for others it may involve a code word or time out card which lets people know that they need to leave. The key is to remember that this is just one activity. One size doesn't fit all. If it doesn't work, there will be other opportunities and other activities which may be a better fit.

Those of you who follow me in other places will know that I am a *big fan* of praise and reinforcement. Even as adults we like to be told that we are doing a good job and our children are no different. The key here should be that the praise and reward is for trying rather than succeeding. It should be given even if your child has only managed to step through the door. Ensure they know you understand what a big step that is and how proud you are of them just for trying.

Helping Your Child To Sleep

I'm often asked by parents who are getting very little sleep what advice I can give them, to make nighttime a little less stressful for everyone involved. When experts get involved the standard advice is to have a settled bedtime routine, with all electronic devices turned off for an hour before bed. Whilst that is undoubtedly good advice, it rarely gets to the route of the problem.

In many cases it is about as useless as telling parents to get their children to count sheep. And ultimately it leaves parents feeling as if no-one really understands what is actually happening. The reality is it is rarely that simple. In my experience there are three main causes of children and young people struggling to sleep. This chapter aims to address each and suggest strategies that may help some children. It isn't a magic wand, but I hope if nothing else it will make you feel a little less alone.

Lack of Melatonin

Many children with Autism struggle to drift off to sleep at night. For some this is because their bodies aren't producing Melatonin naturally. Melatonin can be prescribed via a paediatrician (via GP) or psychiatrist (via CAMHs) and is given before bed as part of the bedtime routine. A small dose is usually prescribed initially, which is then upped if needed. It is extremely weight dependent so don't be surprised if it stops working when your child has a growth spurt. You may need to go back to be reassessed.

Anxiety about being alone

Some children and young people find it very difficult to sleep because they are worried about being alone. Because of difficulties with theory of mind, not being able to physically see the person caring for them can provoke high levels of anxiety. The state of hyperarousal caused by the feelings of anxiety can not only make it difficult for children and young people to fall asleep at night but can also mean they struggle to get back to sleep if they wake during the night.

What can you try:

- ✓ A social story about sleeping and where everyone is during the night is a good place to start. This should be read at least once a day over an extended period of time, with some children it will continue to be read each night before bed. Incorporating the child's special interest will help maintain their interest in the story and enhance the likelihood of them retaining the message.

- ✓ Try putting a photograph on your bedside table of them and a photo of you on theirs. Ideally within the photographs you should both be in your own beds sleeping. The photograph will act as a visual reminder that you are still where you should be. But knowing you are also looking at them as they sleep will also help them to feel reassured.

- ✓ A calm pack, containing their favourite calming items can also be useful. The pack should be easily accessible on their bedroom table and contain things like photographs of you having a nice time as a family. A stuffed toy and something that is non-stimulating yet special interest related is also helpful. Each night write a new note to your child and put it in the calm pack, that way if they wake they are able to have contact with you and feel your presence without physically waking you.

- ✓ Using a baby monitor in reverse can allow your child to physically see you and can make a big difference to some children. Put the baby monitor in your room so that your child can see you if they wake briefly in the night. The sight of you sleeping in your bed may be enough to help them settle and go back to sleep. For older children (or if you don't fancy the invasion of a baby monitor watching your every move) walkie talkies may do the trick… Though of course the beeping of you will still wake you, the fact that your child isn't waiting until their anxiety levels have risen then coming into your room, should make it easier for them to fall back asleep more quickly.

Anxiety about the following day

Many children and young people on the Spectrum have very high anxiety levels. It is very common for them to lie awake at night worrying about what will happen the next day, especially if the following day involves change.

What can you try?

- ✓ Allocate some time before bed to allocate worries leaving less pressure on your child when they are trying to sleep.
- ✓ Use a visual timetable (either written or pictorial) as part of your evening routine. Knowing what will happen the following day will help to reduce anxiety about the unknown.
- ✓ Make sure you are as ready as possible for the following day. Ensuring school bags are packed, uniform is ready and lunches (as far as possible prepared) will all help to reduce the number of things to be worried about.
- ✓ Give them a notebook and pen to write down any worries they have during the night, with the reassurance that you will go through them the following morning. The act of writing them down is almost like passing them on to someone else.
- ✓ Work on understanding those worries which regularly occur and work with others involved in the child or young person's life to reduce them. The less anxiety there is during the day, the less there will be at night.

I end this chapter by reminding you that I am a teacher and a mum. I'm not an expert in sleep... if I was I would be getting significantly more of it than I do. But I know from experience that these are things that can help. I hope they help some of you get a little more sleep.

And if not then I remind you that you are not alone, and that one step at a time you will get there.

Tackling Personal Hygiene

Personal hygiene is something lots of children and young people struggle with. After all playing computer games or watching TV is far more exciting than taking a shower or brushing your teeth.

Add into the mix the sensory difficulties of many children on the Spectrum and the need to stay in control experienced by those with Pathological Demand Avoidance and it isn't surprising that creating good personal hygiene routines can be a particular challenge for many families of children with Autism.

So, if this is an area that your child finds difficult, what can you do?

- ✓ **Implement a reward scheme**

    I know it's something I talk about a lot, but particularly in the early stages of setting up something difficult a new a well thought out reward scheme really can make a difference. Think carefully about what will be most motivating for your child, a small reward after each incident of personal care or a chart working towards something larger that means more to them.

    Once a good routine has been established, rewards can very gradually be faded, to make self care a more natural part of the day.

- ✓ **Think about how you can make the sensations easier**

    Trial different sponges and cloths, different types of toothbrushes, different types of towels and baths versus showers. Discuss with your child which of these is less annoying and frustrating. It is for instance easy for us as parents to assume that a shower will be less irritating for our children because it takes less time, whereas for some the sensation of the water falling on their skin will be physically painful in a way that a bath may not be.

    The key is to involve your child in the activities and show them that you understand that it is hard. Listen carefully to what they tell you and demonstrate through your actions that you are taking them seriously and doing all you can to make it as easy as possible.

✓ **Make them feel special**

Take them shopping – ideally at a quiet time – so it is a treat rather than something to become anxious about – to choose their own self care products. Allow them to choose products with smells that appeal to them, and a wash bag to keep their products together that they like. Having products that young people have picked out themselves makes them much more likely to feel in control and therefore to want to use them.

✓ **Explain the reasons**

If there is something that many of my students struggle with it's strong smells. Most of us avoid wearing perfume for this reason, and there is always a packet of mints in the drawer in case our breath causes offence. Relating their own personal hygiene to the smells your child finds offensive can be helpful in showing them just why personal hygiene is so important. For some children you may need to amplify this a little by spending a weekend practicing poor hygiene yourself. Photographs, which can be found online, of teeth that have become rotten can also be helpful. Using these these practical examples, it's much easier to be able to explain just why personal care is something that you nag about. The key is to show them that there is a reason behind your nagging, you are not just nagging for the sake of being annoying.

✓ **Make it fun**

Whether it's using a timer, or competing with a sibling to see whose teeth are the cleanest at the end of the week adding a sense of challenge or competition can really help some young people. For others social stories directly related to their special interest are the key behind adding an element of fun, whilst for others being able to listen to their favourite music whilst taking a bath, or using products that will colour the water are the key. From fizzing bath bombs, to crayons to use in the tub there are a whole host of exciting products out there. For younger children in particular, distraction often plays a successful part in establishing a personal hygiene routine, so finding the fun trick that makes it worthwhile for your child to take part can be really helpful. You may have to try several before you hit on the right one for your family.

✓ **Try using a schedule or tick sheet**

Making a set time for personal hygiene to take place can take some of the nagging out of the situation, and therefore reduce the pressure. For some young people a physical schedule or tick sheet of activities which need to be done in the morning or after school will help with this. For others just knowing that it will happen at the same time every day will be enough. Thinking carefully about the time of day can also make a difference. In our house showers happen straight after school, before any preferred activities happen. Straight after shower comes snack and iPad time, meaning that the non-preferred activity is instantly followed by preferred ones. For us that definitely reduces the amount of arguments caused.

When it comes to personal hygiene, as with so much else, there are times when picking your battles is key; especially if sensory sensitivities are involved. For some children products like dry shampoo and chewable toothbrushes can help on those days when you know that a demand - however reasonable - is going to be too much to handle.

Ways To Make Homework Less Stressful

If there is one thing that I hate equally as both a mum and a teacher, it has to be homework. For many of my students, and indeed my daughter, making the crossover from school to home can be challenging. It can be extremely difficult for them to understand why we would want them to complete school work at home. But with a little bit of creativity, from both parents and teachers it is possible to make homework less stressful for students with Autism.

My top tips for making homework less stressful:

→ **Assess the task**

As a teacher I can testify to the fact that keeping parents happy when it comes to homework is a completely impossible task. No matter how much work you set there will be some parents who want more and some who want less. Most teachers are however more than willing to have an open dialogue with parents. If a task doesn't feel relevant to your child, go and talk to the staff involved. Ask whether they can limit the amount of tasks sent home, and ensure that only those that are essential to their learning are set.

Do not be afraid to be honest about how difficult your child finds homework. Most teachers receive very little training in Autism. And what can seem like ambivalence is often lack of knowledge. Openness is the best way to promote better understanding and ensure that your child gets what they need.

→ **Explore other options**

Discuss whether there are times during the school day when doing homework may be more suitable than bringing it home. Experience tells me that for many students with Autism, completing homework at breaktimes, lunchtimes and at after school homework clubs is much less stressful than doing so at home. It won't be the right answer for everyone, which is why open dialogue between parents and teachers is so important.

But for some, completing the work at school (where the work belongs), with access to the member of staff who set it (to reduce the anxiety about getting it wrong), and using the same equipment the piece of work was started with can greatly reduce the stress surrounding it.

→ **Think about equipment**

One of the major issues we have with homework in our house, is when it involves completion of a piece of work that has already been started. It can be really difficult for students to break off from work and start again. But if this transition between places involves using different equipment, even if that is just a different pencil, that can greatly add to the stress. Although it may seem unimportant and even unidentifiable to you, many children on the Spectrum will be able to differentiate between subtle shades of difference in lead or ink. This lack of perfection can make it extremely difficult to complete the task. Having an open dialogue between home and school can ensure that children will have access to the same equipment in both places in these cases.

→ **Set a specific amount of time**

It isn't unusual, in a quest for perfection, for children to spend a very long time on a piece of work. This can mean that what a teacher intended to take five minutes, can expand to take the whole weekend. In some cases this can be because a student is determined that every word in every sentence is perfect. In others it's about detail. And in others can mean that although a student is trying to work they sit paralysed unable to complete the first word. Open dialogue between school, the student and parents can ensure everyone knows how long should be spent on a particular task. This should be stuck to by everyone. Even if it means the task itself is incomplete. If homework starts to take over the entirety of family time, stress will increase. This in turn will further affect both academic performance and emotional wellbeing. It needs to be guarded against.

→ **Ensure explanations are clear**

There is nothing worse as a student or as a parent, than having battled homework, to be told the task is wrong or needs to be redone. Young people with Autism often focus on detail, and can find seeing the bigger picture hard. It is therefore essential that careful written instructions accompany each task that is sent home. This ensures that parents are able to guide the task at home.

It's essential that communication happens early in a child's school career to determine how this will happen. The earlier a child is successful at homework the more likely they are to be willing to attempt it again.

→ **Start small and break work down**

Be realistic about all tasks. Ensure that communication is always open. Ensure that any task that is set and attempted gives the student the maximum chance of success. Breaking tasks down, by using writing prompt cards is an excellent way of doing this. These mean that an extended piece of written work can be broken down into two sentence chunks, which makes it feel more achievable for both parents and students.

Can we really make homework less stressful?

Honestly, yes. We can reduce it, but we are unlikely to eliminate the stress totally. We need to recognise that even using all of these strategies, homework is likely to be difficult and stressful both for you and your children. There are likely to be times when it simply doesn't happen, despite everyone's best efforts and intentions. As parents don't be afraid to talk openly to teachers about the difficulties involved with completing tasks. If you don't talk to them, they are unlikely to realise just how hard it can be.

Revision Tips That Will Make Life A Little Easier

If there is one thing that many of my of my most academically able students struggle with, it's the idea of revision. Revision feels alien to many for two reasons, firstly it means going over and over something that you have already done, and secondly it brings with it the added pressure of the expectation that most revision occurs at home. Add to this the anxiety about impending exams, which in themselves mean dealing with the unexpected and handling change and it isn't surprising that most would rather do anything other than revise.

What can we do as parents, to make the process more manageable?

- ✓ **Think about their learning style**

    Do they prefer to read or listen? Given a choice would they draw or watch a video? Taking their learning style into account and coming up with different ways to demonstrate their knowledge using methods they enjoy is far more likely to encourage them to explore it.

- ✓ **Try iMovie**

    iMovie is currently the app of choice in our house, and the opportunities it offers is endless. Why not encourage your child to make an iMovie trailer about the topic they need to revise. The app provides the structure, meaning that they only need to think about the content. Once they have made a video about the topic they can watch it repeatedly until they feel confident about the information.

- ✓ **Get out the index cards**

    For visual learners index cards can be a great choice. Encourage young people to fill them with written notes or diagrams and organise them in different areas of the house. Picturing the area of the house where the index cards were displayed will help them to recall the information on them.

✓ **Use the voice record feature**

Recording their own notes and playing it through headphones on a phone or tablet can really help some young people to focus on learning. Perfect for kinaesthetic learners who benefit from movement whilst learning and for listening to in a dark room for those who need to only focus on one thing thing to retain information.

✓ **Rearrange Post-it notes**

Actively moving different parts of a sequence can make a difference to some young people. Looking at a list is often not enough to enable a young person to memorise it. Physically moving and sticking the Post-it notes into the right order can help both with making the revision process more interesting and with remembering the information.

✓ **Make them the expert**

Asking a young person to test you on the information can really help make revision a more interesting prospect. It can also help to really reduce the pressure that they would feel if you reversed things by testing them. They can keep out their notes or text books and devise questions to test your knowledge – improving their own by checking to see if you have the right answer.

✓ **Make trading cards**

Top Trumps style trading cards can be a great way to learn facts and figures in a bid to stay on top of the game. Perfect for young people who love to draw or to learn through games, this is a revision style guaranteed to bring hours of fun.

✓ **Cut up exam style questions**

The very sight of a full exam paper can be enough to get anxiety levels spiralling, yet for many young people with Autism practicing the wording of the questions is key. Cutting up papers and putting individual questions into a jar, then selecting one to answer each time they feel up to it can be a great way to both reduce anxiety about the papers themselves and to practice the question style.

✓ **Practice making a mark scheme**

Many young people struggle to work out the level of detail that questions are looking for. Giving them a piece of text about their special interest and asking them to create a set of questions based on it and a mark scheme to go with those questions can be a great way of teaching the skill. Children will be engaged by the subject matter, less anxious than when they are put on the spot in an exam and will be able to start to understand how an examiner thinks. For those who struggle to write the level of detail required this can make a huge difference.

The trick with revision as with so many other things is to personalise it. Feel free to tweak these strategies and add to them. Making revision something your child wants to do, rather than feeling as though you should stick to traditional methods is far more likely to enable them to truly be #UNIQUEANDSUCCESSFUL.

The Challenge Of Christmas

December provides more challenges than usual for many children with Autism. Both at school and at home there are changes galore. There are loud noises, crowded places, a multitude of 'fun' activities and lots of very excited peers. What's more at this time of year, we not only expect our children to cope but to be happy about doing so.

This chapter therefore contains a handy list of issues to prepare for and ways to make surviving December a little less stressful.

Father Christmas

We spend our entire year telling our children to avoid strangers. Then suddenly December rolls around and we expect them to talk and even hug a strange man in a big red suit, who looks slightly different every time he is seen. For our children, who so often live by rules it can be difficult to comprehend just why we want them to change the way they act. And for some children even the thought of seeing Father Christmas can be too much. Warning children in advance, using schedules to prepare for visits and asking children what they would feel comfortable with are all steps in the right direction. Some children cope better seeing him in groups than they do alone, and for others giving them an alternative option whilst siblings or classmates visit alone is the best option. The key is to listen to the individual child and not to force them into the activity if it would cause more distress than pleasure.

School plays and nativities

At this time of year, particularly in primary school the usual timetable and carefully structured school day is often altered beyond recognition. And whilst for some children this can be a source of pleasure, for others it is a cause of immense frustration as the cornerstones of the school day shift. Preparing children for what will happen is key. Using schedules will make a big difference as will talking to teachers in advance so that you can help prepare children for the changes that will take place.

As in every case the needs of the child should come first, and for some children this may mean that an effort needs to be made to ensure that at least parts of their school day are kept as normal as possible. Remember that differentiation doesn't begin and end in lessons, some children may find being on stage too overwhelming yet love being involved with the lighting or costume elements of the production. Communication with the school is key to success.

Christmas parties

Christmas parties can be noisy, they can be busy, and they often involve at least some element of controlled (or uncontrolled chaos). Many involve the wearing of unfamiliar itchy clothes and being surrounded by unfamiliar people. Whilst some children will love them, for others they will cause a great deal of anxiety. Agreeing on an outfit and trying it on in advance, talking about quiet places where children can escape to if needed and noise reducing tools like ear defenders can all help. Above all ensure children are aware of what will happen at the event and have a plan for a positive way forward if things don't quite go to plan.

Presents

Presents can be hard, because by their nature presents incur high expectations for all of us. Dealing with managing these expectations for children who find change difficult can be extremely difficult. Dealing with the reactions of a child who believes in honesty can also result in challenges both for parents and present givers alike. Being open and honest about your child's needs, their likes, dislikes and interests can be key to ensuring success. Clearing space pre-Christmas for new items can also help to reduce anxiety about the arrival of new items and how these may change the look of a room. For those with older children with the ability to do so, practicing scripts for non-preferred presents can also be helpful in making them feel less concerned about what will happen on the day.

Christmas Day

Christmas Day is busy, it's bustling, it's full of excitement. It's also completely different to any other day of the year. Family members pop in and out (sometimes invited and sometimes not), the TV schedule changes completely, and even the food is totally different. For those children who enjoy routine, it can be a hard balance between ensuring the day is settled and avoiding a Meltdown. Schedules can help a lot for preparing children for what the day itself will look like, as can giving them somewhere quiet to escape to if needed.

The key is to remember that the day *doesn't have to look a set way, it can in fact look any way that you and your family want it to.*

Preparing A Child To Return To School After The Holidays

My experience as a teacher tells me that when it comes to returning to school after the holidays children with Autism tend to fall into one of two groups. The first group, can't wait to get back. They've enjoyed being at home for the holidays but crave the structure and routine that being back at school brings. It's a chance to be reunited with friends and an end to the chaos that the holiday season brings.

The second group, find the return to school much more difficult. They have had time at home, where relatively few demands have been placed on them. They have enjoyed directing their own time and being immersed in their special interests. For this group the idea of returning to school can bring about feelings of anxiety and even anger.

For the purpose of this chapter we will be focusing on this second group and ways that we can reduce the anxiety that they feel about returning to school after a holiday.

Here are my top tips for returning to school:

→ **The weekend before**

Visually show your child on a calendar or schedule when they will be returning to school, then mark off the remaining days. Many children with Autism find time difficult, and being surprised by the return to school can cause additional anxiety. Especially if there are things they were planning to do before the holiday ended that have not yet been done.

Talk to your child about anything they feel that they need to accomplish before returning to school. Whether it's moving up to the next level on their favourite computer game or finishing off the Christmas Cake. Where possible ensure that the things that signify to them that the holiday is over are accomplished in those last few days in order to make the transition easier.

→ **The day before**

Have a relaxing day tying up any loose ends before school begins. Talk to your child about returning to school and any anxieties they have about doing so. Remind them that first day nerves are very normal, but that they have done this before and can do it again. Talking through the timetable for the following day (if you know it) can help to reassure some children that even though there has been a holiday school will still be the same place it was before. For others making a list of things that are worrying them or questions that they have about the new term to be given to their teacher or TA first thing upon arrival can help to reassure them that their concerns are being listened to.

Plan a nice activity for after school together. Nothing major, small and low key but enjoyable works best. It might be time on the computer or a trip to a cafe for cake. Whatever shows your child that you realise that tomorrow will be a hard day for them and that you want to make it a little better.

Follow the usual school night bedtime routine, whatever that looks like in your house. Getting in routine tonight will help in the morning.

→ **The morning**

Give yourself plenty of time to get ready. Don't be surprised if Meltdowns occur as anxiety will be at its highest point. Remaining calm and logical is the best way to react (but you are human and I know from experience doing that as a mum is much harder than as a teacher) so don't beat yourself up if it doesn't go as planned.

A preferred breakfast can help start the day on a good note, as can allowing time to watch a favourite TV show or play a closed ended game. If your child needs time to relax between getting up and leaving the house closed activities tend to work better than open ones as there is a more natural end which tends to be less likely to result in a Meltdown.

If school are in agreement a transition item, such as allowing your child to take a non-expensive present they have been given into school can work to provide a link between the fun they have had during the holidays and returning to school. The excitement of showing off the present to friends and teachers can help to relieve some of the anxiety about stepping over the door.

Be as positive as you can be. Whilst it's important to always recognise your child's worries and anxieties about returning to school and you should be supportive of those. It's also critical that you remain positive (even if you don't feel it). Your child will take cues from you, so ensure you reassure them repeatedly that they can do this and have a good day.

→ **Once at school**

Starting the day on a positive note is really important. Where possible ensure that a preferred member of staff is waiting outside the building to greet your child and guide them to their classroom.

Encourage the teacher to make the first activity a preferred one, where possible ensure it is related to their special interest. This doesn't mean the teacher can't teach their normal lesson. If they are planning to teach apostrophes, there's nothing to stop them doing so whilst writing about a Disney Film. Or perhaps they are focusing on habitats, in which case why not relate it to Pokemon. The key is to try to add at least a little bit of personalisation.

Remember that just walking through the door and staying in class will be hard for some students. Demands should be kept to a minimum and all positive behaviours should be reinforced. Demands can gradually be built up as the week progresses and your child settles back in school.

Communicate with teachers both about how the day has gone and about any anticipated changes in the coming term. If the day has been a challenging one remember to focus on what has been achieved as well as what has gone wrong.

→ **After school**

Reduce demands as much as possible, allowing your child to participate in preferred activities where possible.

Focus on what has gone right at school and how to build on that tomorrow, rather than on what hasn't gone as planned.

Continue with a normal school night bedtime routine.

Although first days are often challenging, the good news is that as young people get older these tend to get easier. Be kind to yourself, and try to arrange some time you can relax after the drop off or pick up is complete. Remember that you can't give from a glass that is half empty, and that it's ok to need some time to recover from days that are fraught with anxiety.

Helping Children And Young People To Understand Emotions

There is nothing that causes my daughter more anxiety than feeling as though people are upset with her. The reality is through that on at least 90% of the occasions she worries she isn't in trouble at all. It's a story I see reflected in my students, who all too often come back from class convinced that the teacher is unhappy with them simply because they didn't smile. It's instances like these that remind me just why working on understanding the emotions of others is so important.

How to help with understanding emotions:

→ **Cartoons are a great place to start**

Cut out pictures of your child's favourite cartoon characters with different expressions on their face. Then talk about, sort, or label them with their emotions. Cartoons are a great place to start because their expressions are much clearer than those of people and therefore easier to understand. Crucially they are also more motivating, especially if you can relate them to your child's special interest, but also because their success rate is much higher in the early days. (If you have an older child try looking at Manga characters or Pokemon in order to keep the activity age appropriate).

→ **Once cartoons are mastered, photos of your child are a great next step**

Where possible photos should be taken naturally in a range of different environments to help with generalisation. Sitting a child there and asking them to demonstrate emotions is unlikely to work – as when they look at the photographs and talk about them with you they will know they weren't feeling the feelings you are discussing. Photographs can be sorted, put on a display on the wall, or popped into an emotions book and labelled. The key is the discussion around them though, rather than the end product that is reached.

→ **Next comes friends and family**

At this stage things start to become difficult and you should expect some resistance, especially from those young people who struggle with making mistakes. They know that this is a task that they will find hard and that they will get wrong. Doing the initial activities will help to build their confidence and they should be done even if you feel they are tasks that have already been mastered for this very purpose. But this stage should be approached gently and with a reward scheme for participation firmly in tact.

Start with easy emotions, such as happy and sad and build up gradually from there adding one emotion at a time. Focus at this stage on facial reactions that look like the emotions being felt. Where possible try to remove any external factors to involvement, e.g. If you know a child struggles with writing have labels pre-made, and if you know a young person finds doing things with an audience around hard, make sure that it is just you and them.

→ **Move on to drama**

For this activity drafting in other family members is key. Although you should start with simple straightforward emotions and scenarios once these are mastered these should be extended. The key at this stage is to explore how sometimes different faces can mean quite different things. Act out various scenarios and explain how you were feeling in each one, whilst also explaining the look on your face.

Good scenarios to work through include things like:

- A teacher looking miserable in a classroom – student thinks they are cross with them, but the teacher is worried about their child who is poorly at home.
- A teenager is waiting for a bus whilst politely chatting and smiling to an old lady, but actually feeling bored.

- A child is opening a birthday present containing a gift they already have but looking delighted on the surface.

→ **...and then to TV shows and films**

Again using preferred shows is likely to increase the amount of buy in from young people. The key here is that scenes can be played and replayed to explore ideas, yet children and young people get to practice on a much wider range of faces and scenarios than can ever be created.

Watching a film is in many ways like practicing in real life, but without the pressure and with the ability to rewind whenever needed. It's also easy to keep learning fresh and new, whilst still ensuring plenty of repetition.

→ **Lastly generalise to real life scenarios**

Once young people feel confident and comfortable, it's much easier to extend the skills that have been learnt to real life scenarios. At this point you can begin discussing and asking children how they think people feel around them and start to explore how that affects our behaviour, before going on to discuss the impact of their actions on the feelings of others – both positive and negative.

It's a long journey, so don't be disheartened if you don't see progress overnight. The key is to be patient, to move slowly through the stages and at all times to ensure a high rate of success. *You can do this and so can your children.*

Strategies To Help Young People Who Mask

Just like everyone else children and young people with Autism react to stress and anxiety in different ways. Some react instantly and with those children it's easy to see what the triggers are. This means it's much much easier for those around them to both understand and solve the problem. Others however, are able to keep a neutral face whilst being in inward turmoil.

Those are the children, whose stress levels gradually build throughout the day, yet have no release. The ones who get to a point where they explode over what looks like nothing. The ones who often look 'fine' all day at school, yet get home and their world falls apart. Because once they feel safe there is no more need to mask. No more need to look as though they are coping. The anxiety which has accumulated must be let out, and bewildered parents are often left wondering what on earth happened to cause the Meltdown they are seeing before their eyes.

What can we do to make a difference?

→ **Firstly, it's crucial that parents and teachers work together**

Just because the Meltdowns occur at home, does not mean that it's a home problem. All too often schools look at a student who is seemingly coping well during the day and assume that the issues are with parenting or home. The reality is the truth is quite often the opposite. Young people with Autism who mask are often followers of rules, they know the strict code of conduct expected in school and do not want to get into trouble. They will follow the rules at any cost to themselves, until they arrive home. Only once they are somewhere they feel totally safe will they allow their true feelings out. The best way to help these children and young people is through a truly co-ordinated approach.

→ **Find the triggers**

If you haven't already completed the tracking sheets (link on page 146) then this is the time to do so. Every aspect of your child's day should be looked at for potential triggers. Talking to them when they are calm and feel safe can often be the best time to identify these. Some children find it easier to make a list whilst others find it easier to discuss things with a trusted adult. The key is to reassure them that you genuinely want to know which things they find hard and want to help them. They need to understand that they will not be in trouble.

→ **Consider the environment**

Sensory issues can often play a huge part in anxiety levels, and for some these can be difficult to identify. Some young people will be able to tell you that they find it hard to concentrate whilst the lights are bright or that the breeze coming through the classroom door is distracting. Others may only be able to tell you that their head or eyes hurt by the end of the day. Sometimes finding the contributing factors is a little like putting together a jigsaw puzzle. You have to try lots of pieces until you find the ones that fit.

→ **Work on ways of enabling the young person to recognise their own emotions building**

Teaching your child strategies like how to ask for time out when needed, how to scale their emotions or how to colour and recognise their feelings can all be helpful. Doing these activities as a whole family, rather than signalling your child out can be particularly helpful as they can help children to realise that we all feel anxious at times and need to develop ways of coping. Normalising their feelings will help them to feel less worried about opening up when there is a problem and help them to see that they don't need to mask their true feelings.

→ **Talk to school about providing a place where your child feels safe to be themselves during the day**

For some children and young people the act of being surrounded by people all day can be a big cause of the build up of their anxiety. Giving them time throughout the day to be by themselves or with a smaller number of people can make a huge difference. This could be accomplished by the use of a dark den or tent, a quiet room, or by giving the option to stay inside at lunch or break times to build Lego or play on a computer. We often feel that we should encourage children with Autism to engage with others during social times. But we forget that we are already asking them to do a lot of this during lesson time. Following the lead of the child is important, sometimes time to themselves can make a world of difference.

→ **Create a way of communicating between home and school**

Develop a quick and easy way to communicate between home and school so that both you and your child's teachers are always in the loop about anything that has happened. This may work best through a home school diary, through quick emails back and forth with key information about the day or previous evening, or via a quick phone call. Deciding on the method should not only be about what is most convenient, but about what is most effective. A home school diary may be the easiest method, but a downside can be that the child has often been at school or home for several minutes before the diary is read. A phone call can mean the child is greeted differently and offered a different task on arrival at home or school depending on the day that has been had.

→ **Building trust is essential**

If you are expecting your child to open up to you about their anxieties and feelings, you need to ensure that you react in the right way consistently. Do not diminish their worries, take them seriously and ask how you could make it easier for them to handle it. This doesn't necessarily mean giving them permission not to do the task, but it does mean working with them to find ways to make that task less stressful.

So if a child or young person tells you that writing at school is a major cause of their anxiety for example, you can look at ways to make that easier. For some an alternative way of recording, such as dictating into an iPad or typing on a computer may

STRATEGIES

help, for others breaking down the task into more manageable chunks using a writing frame or writing prompt cards may help. Whereas for others it may be that using ear defenders or listing to music when they do extended written work helps them to focus rather than being distracted by the classroom. The key is to ensure that your child knows that you will help. You don't need to have all of the answers, but you do need to show them that you will keep trying and fighting their corner until you develop a solution that works.

→ **Arriving home**

Taking the lead from your child when they arrive home from school can be key. Sometimes with children that mask the normal rules don't apply. You may need to allow for an hour of video games, or an hour relaxing listening to music or watching TV before placing any demands upon them. With younger children, time to run at the park or in the garden may help them to burn off some of the anxiety they are feeling. Or they may just want to be by themselves after a day of being surrounded by others.

Space and time are likely to be key in helping them to decompress after a challenging day. Try to resist the urge of asking them what is wrong, instead let them know that you will be there for them when they need you (with my mum head on, I know that this is much easier said than done).

Above all, be kind to yourself. The reaction when they arrive home is because they feel safe with you, because they can be themselves. It is not because you are doing anything wrong. Eat chocolate, buy cake and remember that you will get through this.

When it comes to helping children and young people that mask we have to be all the more creative. Help via the traditional EHCP route often takes much longer to achieve than for young people who display their emotions at school. That doesn't mean however, that support can't be put in place, but it's more likely you'll need to be super proactive in educating your child's school about the ways they can help - even without an additional budget. And that's where what you have learnt in this chapter comes in. Remember you are the expert in your child, you can do this,

Managing Meltdowns

Once a Meltdown has begun, it is very difficult to stop it. Instead what we often need to do is to allow it to run its course in a manner that is as safe as possible for all concerned. This section of the book focuses on simple strategies to help you to manage Meltdowns throughout the run up, the Meltdown itself and after the Meltdown has finished.

A Meltdown is on the way

As parents of children on the Spectrum, we often develop a sixth sense for an impending Meltdown. We can see it coming, yet we're not always sure how to stop it in it's tracks.

If you find yourself in this position you can give the following a try:

- ✓ Give your child time to immerse themselves in their special interest (this will release endorphins that will help them to relax).

- ✓ Give them some time alone to relax (In our house we use lying on a bed with a book, but any relaxing activity that means your child isn't under pressure to interact will work just as well).

- ✓ Depending on the child, well timed humour can work well. Things like remembering a funny situation where the child laughed are particularly effective. (In our house, laughing at me works well).

- ✓ Avoid getting into arguments, your child is likely to be somewhat argumentative at this point (you can deal with any of the points they raise later - but now is not the time to do so). Phrases like 'I'm so sorry that I upset you', 'I'm really sorry you feel that way', 'I'm sorry I made you feel that way', 'How can I help make that easier for you?' can be helpful to have in the back of your head. This way you can acknowledge your child's feelings and worries without tackling them head on.

- ✓ Stay as calm as you can (easier said than done I know - especially if you are somewhere that you really don't want a Meltdown to happen.
- ✓ Offer them some time out, away from the situation that is upsetting them.

Once a Meltdown has started you often need to let it run its course, however there are things you can do to make sure it doesn't become bigger than it otherwise would be.

During the Meltdown itself:

- ✓ Avoid giving instructions or asking questions. This can make an already overwhelming situation feel unbearable and really escalate the Meltdown.
- ✓ With almost all children limiting your verbal language as much as possible is the best strategy you can use. During a Meltdown young people are only able to process around 10% of what they hear properly, and therefore can become easily confused by what you are saying.
- ✓ Don't try to reason with the arguments that are thrown at you, at this moment reasoning won't work. As above phrases like 'I'm so sorry that that upset you', 'I'm really sorry you feel that way', 'I'm sorry I made you feel that way', 'How can I help make that easier for you?' can help make children feel listened to without further escalating the situation.
- ✓ Keep calm, sometimes removing yourself from the situation (as long as your child is safe), is the easiest way to do this. (I'm much better at calm with my teacher head on than I am with my mum head on).
- ✓ Give your child somewhere safe they can go, somewhere they can say whatever they need to, insult the world and swear without sanctions. Whether that's their bedroom, a small den set up for the purpose or outside in the garden - whatever you feel would work best in the environment you have.

- ✓ A pen and paper can be really helpful for some young people, that way they can use it to write down their thoughts and feelings. Afterwards they can decide whether to show it to you, so that you can answer (on paper works best) or tear it up and bin it as a way of getting rid of the worries.

Whatever happens during the Meltdown, do not talk about sanctions at this point. I believe in sanctions - now just isn't the right time to talk about them.

After a Meltdown:

- ✓ After a Meltdown is a great time to talk to your child.
- ✓ Reassure them that you love and care about them. The likelihood is that they will respond in kind, which will help both of you feel a little better, especially if hurtful things have been said during the Meltdown.
- ✓ Once they are fully calm, it can be a fantastic time to talk about how you can help them better next time they feel a Meltdown happening, and also what they could do differently to help themselves.
- ✓ Now is the time to discuss any consequences that may be needed, for instance if they have hurt someone or broken something during the Meltdown. (See section on consequences for more information on how to do this).
- ✓ Look back and evaluate yourself. What were the triggers? What if anything could you do differently next time?

Most importantly be kind to yourself. *You are human.* Even if things could have been done differently do not beat yourself up. Evaluate yourself not to bring blame, but to make next time easier. Make a cup of tea, have a bar of chocolate and breathe. You did a good job.

Rewards Matter

I am a firm believer in both rewards and sanctions. Quite simply because, both exist (implicitly and explicitly in the real world), and part of our job as parents and teachers is to prepare our children for that world. The question I always ask both of myself and others, is whether we would go to work without reward. The likelihood is, that most of us wouldn't. Yet everyday we expect our children to do just that.

For children on the Spectrum rewards are particularly important. They find many aspects of what we expect of them difficult. Showing them that we recognise the efforts they put into tackling those things is a crucial part of building their self esteem and giving them tangible proof that they are successful. The key however, is matching the right reward scheme to the right child, especially if the child has Pathological Demand Avoidance or demand avoidant tendencies. Crucially all schemes should be about the child. They should feel like they are working towards something they want, because they want to do so. Not because it is a way of pleasing the adults around them.

They should also always be incremental. And by this I mean that tokens or points shouldn't be lost or taken away for unwanted behaviour. Schemes that involve for instance 5 consecutive days of the desired action and/ or behaviour should also be avoided. Schemes like these become easy ways for young people to sabotage their success and cause more distress than help. I have lost count of the number of students I have seen who have kept Friday afternoon Golden Time until Friday morning, then at the last minute lost everything. A flexible system makes self sabotage much harder, because that would mean that although Golden Time didn't happen on Friday, it would occur on Monday - the 5th day of the desired actions/ behaviours - and thus still give the young person that sense of success.

The scheme you use will depend upon your child, their age and their level of understanding. If the first one doesn't work try another. When it comes to rewards, one size definitely does not fit all.

These are my favourites:

→ **Token boards**

Token boards are most useful for very young children or those with limited language. They are perfect for encouraging task completion or for encouraging positive behaviours over a short period of time. The most successful token boards are based on a child's individual interests. So for a child who loves Thomas The Tank Engine drawing a railway track on a piece of A4 paper and laminating it forms an excellent base. Then print of a selection of between 5 and 15 of your child's favourite engines to become the tokens. Because the child is invested in the tokens as well as the overall prize, their chances of success are maximised. Printing off images of a selection of small rewards to put at the end of the board will also help as this provides a visual reminder of what success means.

Rewards can include anything from TV time, to snacks, from a game of chase to time spent on an electronic device. The important factors are that it must be something which the child will find rewarding, it must be available immediately and it must be tangible. Once a child has gained all of their tokens they should be allowed to immediately claim their reward.

→ **Spontaneous edible treats**

Although I am well aware that this is an issue that is open to disagreement. I am a big fan of edible treats. In fact at one point a member of staff told me that my classroom resembled Charlie's Chocolate Factory! I like to use them spontaneously rather than as part of an official system. I also choose treats that are deliberately small as this increases the frequency with which I can distribute them without a) giving anyone too much sugar or b) making my life harder through said sugar rush rather than easier.

Edible treats work well when you are out and about, going on a long walk, sitting through long conversations at Grandma's or trying to navigate the shops. For older more streetwise children they also look more socially acceptable, and can be shared with friends if they are around.

→ **Free time**

Everyone likes to be rewarded for their hard work. After all, if you didn't get paid, would you go to work? Take that one step further, if your boss paid you more for accomplishing more, would it make you push yourself even further? So whilst I can't reward my students financially, I like them to know that I recognise when they have done a great job. They are therefore rewarded at the end of each 50 minute lesson with five minutes additional free time for excellent work, and five minutes additional free time for excellent behaviour. It gives them an incentive to work as hard as they can and more importantly it shows them that I have noticed and care that they try hard. This makes them much more likely to want to do so again the next lesson. For those of you looking to share strategies with school, this is one that is cost free and therefore easier to implement on a whole class level than some of the other schemes if teachers (or you) are worried about signalling your child out.

In a home situation, I usually give out extra iPad or TV time; if for instance my daughter has gone out of her way to be helpful, tidied her brother's toys or coped with something particularly stressful.

→ **Tick sheets**

Tick sheets are a more grown up version of token boards, perfect for those young people who like discreet rewards. By popping a small notepad in your pocket, you can add ticks to a page. Once a set number of ticks are achieved the reward is given. This works particularly well on a long day out where you know challenges may occur. The reward should be agreed on beforehand, and the ability to earn ticks should be carried over to the next day and/ or trip out (depending on how you use the scheme) if not enough ticks are achieved on the day.

→ **Praise**

Whilst praise in isolation may not be enough to change behaviour, that doesn't mean it shouldn't be used in addition to other more tangible rewards. Be sensitive though to the needs of the individual, some children love praise to be big, bold and shouted from the roof tops whereas others prefer their praise delivered quietly in a more personal manner. Delivering it in the wrong way can limit and even completely reverse the effect.

→ **Points based systems**

These are best suited for older children who can cope with delayed gratification. Allowing children to collect points over an extended period of time allows them to save up for larger rewards such a cinema trip or new video game. The reward should be agreed on prior to the chart starting and children should visually be able to see their points stacking up as a reminder that they are getting nearer to their target. Points should be rewarded frequently for behaviours that you are trying to encourage.

→ **Reward shops**

These work really well with larger groups or siblings. Having a selection of treats available, each costing a different amount of points means that children have to think about when to trade in their points. The fact that someone else may buy their chosen reward first works as a motivating factor to keep trying hard and to keep saving. Points to spend should be rewarded frequently. I love to tie in the shop points to a child's interest whenever possible Galleons for a child who loves Harry Potter, or gold coins for a Sonic fan both work well.

I end this chapter by reminding you that when it comes to rewards, one size definitely does not fit all. If one system doesn't work try another, and be prepared to tweak, to alter to create a system completely of your own. If you get it right, it will fly. The key is to set it up in a way that means it doesn't become just another demand, and instead is something that excites and intrigues your child: something they want to be part of. Critically if you get it right it will make your life easier, not harder.

Are Consequences Really Needed?

I am a firm believer in consequences, I believe they are part of what teaches us what is right or wrong, and something that our children need to accept happens in the real world. I am not a fan of guilt or recriminations however as I feel both can be damaging and are more likely to cause harm than good.

The best way to introduce the idea of consequences is by sitting together and making a list of family rules. In order for everyone to feel it's fair everyone needs to be involved. Next to the rules should be written a consequence for not keeping the rule. So for instance, the consequence for being unkind to a sibling could be giving an apology, the consequence for violence to another person a technology ban of a specified length. The type of consequences are totally up to you and your family to decide upon. But the key is that they need to be things you are willing to follow through consistently or they won't work effectively.

I like to give young people a chance to earn back some of the time they have lost through good behaviour, as this decreases the chance of them feeling like they have nothing left to lose and helps to reduce the chance of a Meltdown when a consequence is delivered. So if you give for example a five day technology ban, for each good day, a day is taken off the end of the ban. Effectively meaning it can be reduced to 2.5 days if good choices are made. If you haven't used consequences before it will feel alien at first for you and your children and you will need to persevere through some challenging behaviour before they realise you are serious about sticking to the rules. But once they know you will apply them consistently and fairly, it will get easier.

When one of the rules is broken, it will usually be because your child is upset, their anxiety levels are high or they are mid Meltdown. During a Meltdown is not the time to deliver consequences or even to discuss them. Instead wait until your child is totally calm and when they are sit them down to talk. Ask them what went wrong and what they would do differently next time. Then refer them to the list of family rules, and ask them what they think should happen next.

By using the rules, the consequence will feel less personal, which is really important. When they tell you what the consequence should be, agree with them and apologise letting them know you understand it will be hard. Shouting and recriminations aren't needed.

What If School Isn't Working?

Reducing The Risk Of School Refusal

Quite often when children arrive with me, it's because at some point or another they have become what the system calls a 'School Refuser.' Sometimes that can mean they no longer attend school at all, and in other cases it can mean that attendance becomes increasingly infrequent. In many cases this is a cycle which can be prevented by working together as a team.

The following strategies are designed to reduce that risk from those young people who are likely to refuse to attend school:

→ **Find ways to reduce anxiety in school**

Often anxiety is at the heart of school refusal. Young people feel unable to cope in the placement that they are in, either because of demands (from either people or their environment) or because of the level of sensory overload that they experience whilst they are there. Understanding an individual's anxieties are key. Once a child can talk about what it is about school that is difficult, staff and parents can begin to work to reduce those. Doing so will be different for each child or young person.

For some young people, providing a quiet safe place they can go to in school when they feel unable to be in lesson helps. For others it may be a case of making changes to the timetable to ensure that the day starts with a preferred activity. Whilst for others it may be that regular sensory breaks throughout the day are needed to help them to self regulate and cope with the remainder of the day.

Actively working to reduce those parts of the day which cause the most anxiety needs to be a team effort, between the child, parents and school staff. Working in a unified way will help the child or young person to feel much more secure and listened to.

→ **Ensure days not spent in school are neutral**

It is crucial to make days when your child has refused to attend school as neutral as possible. These days should not result in a punishment but nor should the young person be allowed to engage in preferred activities throughout the whole day. Doing so will increase the desire to stay at home and reinforce that school is not where they want to be. Where possible keep the structure of the day as similar to the school day as you can. Provide simple structured tasks to do in what would be lesson time (even if they are not completed), and limit preferred activities such as mobile phone or console use to when these would be allowed at school.

→ **Develop reward schemes that work - at home and at school**

I am a firm believer that if we ask, a child to do something difficult, they should be rewarded for doing so. I have no problem with positive reinforcement, after all if you were not paid to go to work each day would you do so? With this in mind parents and teachers need to work together with young people to find out what motivates them, and develop a structured reward scheme that feels manageable.

→ **Make sure young people feel successful when they are at school**

When a young person arrives in school they should be welcomed warmly by staff. They should not be asked why they have been missing from school or why they are late. Doing this will only result in them feeling more anxious about returning the time after. Instead ensure that they know that school staff are there for them and will be pleased to see them whenever they feel able to attend.

A big part of this is making sure that whilst they are there they feel wanted, needed and successful. For some young people that may be by giving them small jobs to do, for others it may be by asking them to look after a younger student. Some may appreciate praise about their academic work, others may appreciate a friend coming over to sit with them at lunch.

There is no one size fits all approach. It is all about looking at the individual and understanding what will make them feel successful and wanted within the environment.

→ **Think ahead**

All too often children are left in unsuitable placements for too long. Whilst this is often the result of good intentions in the long term it isn't helpful to them. Once a young person has become a school refuser, especially if this has gone on over a long period, it is much more difficult to get them to attempt a new placement. If something isn't working and there isn't a plan in place that both the school and parents feel will make a significant difference an Emergency Annual Review needs to be called. If outside agencies (e.g. CAMHs) are unable at this point to offer significant and immediate support, the school should admit that they are unable to meet need and ask the authority to look into alternative placements. Meanwhile you as parents need to put consistent pressure on them to do so.

I know I say this often, but when parents and teachers *really work together* in a coordinated manner it is much much easier to secure the best outcomes for children. By sharing knowledge, resources and power they can put things in place that would be ineffective alone in addition to securing support from other services.

Getting Those Who Have Refused School Back Through The Door

There are few issues more complex than school refusal. Even if a school is doing all that they can to support a child during the day, the environment itself can be so challenging that students can feel that they are unable to attend.

So, what can schools and parents do to try to ease them back in through the door?

Arrange a visit out of hours

Sometimes visiting the school building out of hours can feel less overwhelming than visiting during the day. With only teachers and the building to contend with, and the pressures of lessons and other students safely out of the way some students can find this the easiest time to reconnect with school life. Once they have met with their teachers and know that they will be welcoming to them on their return it can make it easier for them to return during the school day without fear of judgement.

Arrange a home visit from a member of staff

For some young people even stepping foot in the door can feel too overwhelming. In these cases a preferred teacher coming on a home visit can help. In some cases more than one visit may be needed. The purpose of these visits should be to build up a relationship between your child and their teacher so that they feel like there is someone in school who cares about them and who they can go to if they have a problem.

Arrange a meeting with friends

Sometimes, especially if children have been away for a while the fear of meeting their peers again can feel like a frightening prospect. Arranging a meet up with a couple of them prior to the return to school can alleviate some of the worries about how they will be treated once they return to school. It can also help to reassure them that nothing at school has changed and that they will be returning to a familiar place with familiar people.

Arrange an escort

Stepping through the front door on your own can be a scary prospect, especially if you've been away for a while. If your child has 1:1 support it may be possible to arrange for their learning support assistant to meet your child at home to help them to reintegrate. If not a peer or someone from your local Autism service may be able to help. The act of someone associated with school coming through their front door can serve to remind them that people care about them and therefore, be a very powerful tool.

Ask the school to send work home

For some young people feeling as though they have missed work and don't know what has been happening whilst they have been away can be a huge cause of their anxiety about returning. The key with work sent home is that it should be sent with an explanation of the lesson and no expectation that it will be completed. Ideally it should be accompanied with a note from the teacher saying something like 'We are really missing you at school and just wanted to let you know what we have been doing. I've sent the work home in case you want to give it a try, but if not don't worry I'll help you when you come back'. It's key that your child knows that they don't have to complete the work in order to return, as otherwise it could become another barrier to their return.

Reduce the timetable

If a full day feels overwhelming, start gradually. This can start off with being in school for as little as five minutes. The key is to build up the time spent gradually and consistently so that the young person knows that they will be spending longer at school each week. Try to avoid for instance doing a term of just mornings as this can become the new normal, making extending the time more difficult. Instead choose your child's favourite lessons. Ask them which part of the week they can cope with and build it up. So week one for instance could be art, week two art and maths, week three art, maths and lunch etc. The key is to involve the young person so that they feel in control of what is happening.

Enabling Successful Reintegration After A Period Of School Refusal Or Exclusion

The sad truth is that for young people with Autism, spending time out of school is more likely than for their neurotypical peers. Schools are busy places, full of rules and restrictions, students need to deal with group work, bustling corridors and peers and teachers who don't always understand them. And that's even before they have to contend with the challenges of a curriculum which isn't designed for differences.

It therefore isn't surprising that this is an environment which many find challenging. And one which, at its most difficult, provokes a flight or fight response. Whether a child is returning to the school environment after an exclusion (either temporary or permanent) or after a period of school refusal it is essential that the school puts steps in place to assist the student in reintegrating as smoothly as possible.

Work as a team

First and foremost it is essential that parents and teachers work together. Open and frank communication between both parties is the best route to achieving the best possible outcomes. It is absolutely essential that parents are treated as equal parties in all decision making. After all, it is you who knows your child the best and you who need to deal with the fall out from any decisions made. If you are totally onboard it will also be much easier for you to explain the reasons behind any decisions to your child in a way that is both convincing and meaningful.

Complete an analysis of students' anxieties and triggers

If a young person has behaved in a way which has resulted in exclusion or has felt unable to walk though the door of school, it is highly probable that anxiety, rather than wilful disobedience, is at the route of the problem. Open dialogue between the student, parents and school staff is the best way to assess exactly what the problem is. It is critical that your child feels listened to. If they are unable to verbalise their worries in a group situation, they should be encouraged to write them or dictate them to a trusted adult.

Once a comprehensive analysis of what causes the young person anxiety has been compiled, a discussion about how these anxieties can be relieved is critical. Sometimes small things like allowing them to use a different entrance or giving them a way out by providing somewhere they can go if things get too much can make a massive difference. Key to this is ensuring that they know that school staff care enough to try to make this placement work.

A fresh start

Whilst particularly in the case of exclusion, especially if physical violence has been involved, emotions of staff involved can run high it is critical that the return is seen as a fresh start. Positivity from all involved is absolutely key to success. Any meetings should focus on ensuring success for your child in the future rather than on what has gone wrong in the past. It is highly likely that if a student's behaviours have become out of control, it is because they have been in a situation where they have been unable to control their emotions. Therefore focusing on giving students strategies to recognise their emotions (e.g. through the use of the Five Point Scale or Zones of Regulation) will be far more successful than talking about sanctions if the behaviours reoccur.

A home visit

For some young people a home visit by a trusted member of staff can prove very important in showing them that school does indeed want them to return. Walking back into a building when you have been absent for a significant period is daunting, and ensuring that some contact is retained can be critical to ensure a student is unable to walk through the door when they are able to return.

Reduce demands

Returning to school after a break can be very challenging for many children, but it can be especially difficult for young people with Autism. It is likely that you will need to reduce demands initially. For some students this will involve substantial changes to their timetable, for others it may involve allowing them to start the school day earlier or later. Sitting down with teachers and your child prior to their return to discuss how this will work in practice is key. Looking at the timetable to identify possible triggers and building in regular sensory breaks will help students to adapt back into the school routine.

Remember reward schemes

Remember that reward schemes are important. Ensure that you show your child that you recognise how hard school is for them and give them the recognition they deserve when things go right. More information about why reward schemes are so important and the different ways they should be implemented for young people with Autism can be found in a previous chapter.

What If School Breaks Down?

The current reality in many authorities is that academically able children with Autism are often difficult to place. There are a multitude of reasons for this, ranging from anxiety about stepping over the door of the building, to behaviours that challenge the status quo.

If you are in this position and struggling to find the right placement for your child, this chapter is worth reading and the ideas within it considered with an open mind.

Primary schools are often easier for children on the Spectrum to thrive in. They are small, contained and have staff that know their children well. It's a sheltered environment where accommodations are easy to make. They are surrounded by children who have grown up with them, and who on the whole are accepting of their differences. For many young people however the transition to secondary school is a hard one.

Mainstream secondary schools are big, they are scary and they are impersonal. Accommodations are often more difficult to make. In addition, for children who are academically able support is often lacking. Added to the mix are noisy corridors, enormous dinner spaces, and a whole host of new children fighting for their place in the pecking order.

Some, learn to thrive in that environment. They find areas that work for them, love having access to more technology and enjoy the fact that if there is a teacher they don't see eye to eye with they can quickly move onto the next lesson. Secondary schools can make inclusion work. And some are committed to doing so. The ones that are exceptional can make a real difference, but the reality is they are few and far between. And even the best may not be able to meet the needs of those children whose anxiety levels are the highest.

Where should you consider?

→ Traditional MLD and SLD schools

These are worth taking a look at and may be appropriate for

some. They are quieter, more controlled environments which are less assaulting on the senses. Staff care deeply about individual pupils and are able to make very individualised accommodations. Most also have fairly extensive Autism experience. The difficulty they face is that their curriculum is often not appropriate. And perhaps more importantly they also often fail to provide an attractive peer group for more academically able students.

→ **EBD schools (Schools For Children With Behavioural Difficulties)**

These are often ones that parents of children with an Autism diagnosis shy away from. However a good EBD school is worth considering. EBD schools are often highly structured environments with clear expectations. They have clear rewards and consequences. Additionally, the children who attend them need lessons providing in an engaging way to keep their interest. Staff are trained to deal with challenging behaviour, and are forgiving in the event of it. They are not the right solution for everyone, and not all of them will be right for children with Autism. However, they are worth looking into.

→ **Privately funded schools**

Local authorities are unlikely to tell you about privately funded options in your area. However, if they can't find a school which meets your child's needs these are an option you can look into and make a case for. This can include privately owned special schools and traditional independent schools. Privately owned special schools are expensive and therefore will be a reluctant choice for most authorities. However, because they are expensive they can also afford to be more flexible, provide more bespoke curriculums and higher levels of support. You will need to make a detailed case about why this is the only setting that can meet your child's needs, but the reality is that at least some of those parents who fight for places receive them. Many authorities do not have enough in authority places, so increasingly they are having to look at other options.

Independent schools can be a double edged sword, but for some families they are the answer. They have small class sizes, and are often both more structured and have higher standards of behaviour than traditional comprehensive schools. This makes them an easier place to succeed for some students on the Spectrum. They are however often lacking in SEND knowledge, and can find behaviour of any kind difficult to deal with. They work best for children who internalise their anxiety, and need to be looked at and spoken to carefully to make sure they are the right place.

→ **Homeschooling or private tutoring?**

For children and young people who are motivated to learn but who struggle in the school environment, homeschooling or private tutoring can prove a good option for some families. It gives the opportunity to completely personalise learning to your child's needs and avoids putting them through the anxiety of a busy school environment. It's an option that will very much depend on family circumstances - one that I'm not sure would work for us (my daughter and I are far too similar) but one that lots of families experience a lot of success with.

→ **A combination approach**

For some children, none of the above will work in isolation and a combination approach is well worth thinking about. This enables a student to split their time between two different settings – or between a school and a more relaxed environment. The reality is the more difficult the child is to place the more flexibility the authority has in placing them.

Don't be afraid to be brave when dealing with your Local Education Authority. Think about what will work for your child and propose it. You may not get it, but on the other hand you just might – especially if it's an option that is cost effective for the authority to make happen.

Final Words

What Is It Really Like In Holland?

There is a very well known poem in special needs circles called 'Welcome To Holland', written by a lady called Emily Perl Kingsley. It's a poem that I first came across when I was just 18 and working at a youth club for children with moderate learning difficulties. It's also one that over the years I have had a love hate relationship with.

The essence of the poem is an analogy where parenting is compared to a journey to a new life. A life that the poet describes as Italy. Except for those of us whose children get a diagnosis of some kind, the idea is that we end up in Holland. The premise is that yes, Holland isn't where we expected to live but that actually there are many beautiful things about Holland - it's a place that is every bit as wonderful to live as Italy.

Today sitting in my somewhat ivory tower, having waved my daughter off happily to do her SATs this morning (a waffle breakfast was promised at school), it's a poem I can relate to. Right now our life is good, really good. There are things we don't do conventionally - crowds are something we try to avoid and germs and bees are both big triggers right now. But on the whole we have found our comfort zone. We are happy and content. Our life works. Holland is a good place to be.

If I skip back five years ago however I felt very, very differently. Life was hard. My daughter had attended two schools and both placements had broken down, she'd also lost vision in one eye due to anxiety and we seemed to spend our whole life driving around and not getting any answers. If you'd asked me back then, I'd have beamed us all back to Italy in a heartbeat.

But the truth is, that just like life in general, wherever you might be in the world and whatever your family dynamics look like, there will be highs and there will be lows. There will be moments you'll want to shout your successes from the rooftops and there will be times you'd quite like to hide under a very large rock.

The world is not a certain one, and neither are our lives. My professional experience tells me that for us the challenges aren't over… right now I'm just enjoying the ride whilst things are good. Soaking up the sunshine and enjoying those moments, storing my energies ready for when they are needed.

This book isn't a magic wand, though if I had one I would happily give it to you in a heartbeat. What I can give you however, is reassurance. Reassurance that you can do this. And reassurance that if right now things are hard, that doesn't mean it will always be that way. Implement one thing at a time, pick your battles carefully and remember you are human.

Conclusion

You Matter Too

Before this book finishes I want to tell you one more story... a story about a very different time in our lives.

Seven years ago I was a single mum.

I was juggling full time teaching in a school for children with social, emotional and behavioural difficulties with simultaneously looking after my daughter. And in those days she found life hard. Incredibly hard. She self harmed frequently and her Meltdowns were a sight to behold. Her diet was very restricted, and our social circle had dwindled to virtually non-existent.

I felt like I was a failure.

I was permanently firefighting. Getting us out of one disaster only for the next to jump up on us. During the day I would run round after my class of eight, and in the evening and on the weekends I would run round after my daughter. When she slept, I marked or planned. Our life outside of home consisted of visits to the cinema to watch Disney Films, and trips to the Lego Discovery centre in the Trafford Centre. We rarely went anywhere else. I had constructed a life that worked for us, a life that didn't add to my daughter's stress levels – or to mine – any more than they needed to be added to.

Because the truth is, I was at breaking point!

Not because of work, or because of my daughter, but because I had lost faith in me. I had lost all sight of who I was as a person and of what I was capable of doing. And then out of the blue I had a conversation on Facebook with a friend I went to university with. Someone who made me realise who I had been, and who I still could be. Someone who reminded me that the girl who believed that anything and everything was possible was buried somewhere inside the woman.

He made me realise that I had to stop letting my life control me, I had to resume control.

So I did three things:

1. I stopped trying to find all of the answers myself. I had spent two years reading everything I could about toddlers and Autism and I felt as though I was going around in circles. Nothing seemed to quite fit what I needed. So I paid privately for consultations with two different people. It was the best money I have ever spent. They gave me a roadmap to follow, which gave me confidence in my decisions and saved me a lot of time.

2. I started eating grown up food. I had got into a rut, of just eating whatever I was cooking for my daughter (which basically consisted of pasta spirals and one brand of cheese) or making a sandwich. Eating real food, made me feel like more of a person again.

3. I bought new knickers. I hadn't bought myself any new clothes since my daughter was born and was pretty much living in my Grandma's hand me downs. Money was tight. Really tight. But I decided that although I couldn't afford new outfits, that wasn't an excuse for wearing knickers with holes in them. I deserved better.

These days life is very different

I'm happily attached, have not just one but two wonderful children that I parent confidently and a job that I adore… I even occasionally remind myself to buy new knickers!

I love that now I get to be that person who helps people believe in themselves. I love that through *Autism Consultancy International* I get to give people the roadmap they need to get back on track. And I love that through our **#UNIQUEANDSUCCESSFUL The Membership** scheme I am able to give ongoing support to families whenever they need it.

Because the truth is you deserve that support. You deserve to have some of the worries lifted off your shoulders and time to spend some time caring for you.

And I want every one of you to remember that you do.

Because I know how hard it is when you are lost and afraid and don't know where to turn. I know so many of you feel isolated and lost right now. But you can do this. Every single one of you.

You can take control and believe in you again.

I am living proof of that.

And you *are* going to be too.

Because this week I want you to take control of one thing in your life. Whether it's joining our free Facebook community **#UNIQUEANDSUCCESSFUL: The Community**, becoming a member of our **#UNIQUEANDSUCCESSFUL The Membership** (details of both can be found over the page) scheme or booking an individual session with me to give you confidence in your decisions, opening the stack of letters waiting by the door, cooking a meal because it's a food you love or replenishing your knicker drawer.

I want you to think about what you need, and I want you to believe you can do this.

Your children believe in you. And I believe in you.

You can do this!

Resources And Further Help

For tracking and analysis sheets please go to:
https://Autismconsultancyinternational.com/talking-Autism parenting-your-unique-child-resources

To our free support community:
#UNIQUEANDSUCCESSFUL: The Community
https://www.facebook.com/groups/169995200363330

To find out more about our membership community:
#UNIQUEANDSUCCESSFUL: The membership
https://Autismconsultancyinternational.com/uniqueandsuccessful-the-membership/

Our membership community is for families just like yours

To discover ways your family can work one to one with Victoria:
https://Autismconsultancyinternational.com/our-packages

About The Author

Victoria is an Autism Specialist, strategy creator, and change maker. She's also the founder and coach at *Autism Consultancy International*. The business was born because she recognised a need for change. A need for a provider that specialises in school aged children, because the truth is that whilst Early Intervention is important, our children's needs don't disappear as they get older.

Instead they change, develop and evolve. And Victoria's aim is to help you and your child's educator(s) develop strategies that grow with them. After spending 20 years working with children and young people on the Spectrum across a range of settings from; home visits; specialist schools, and top ranking independent boarding schools, she has witnessed what happens when young people don't get the support at the right time.

She is also well aware, because she's seen it first hand, just how hard it is to get the right support, even when looking in the private sector. This book and *Autism Consultancy International* is her way of redressing that.

She has a Cambridge University degree in Education and a Post Graduate Certificate in Education from Manchester including three Autism based dissertations. She has also attended numerous Autism based professional courses over the years.

But the truth is, none of that really matters. Because that didn't teach her how to be the teacher and Autism coach she is. That credit goes to the children and young people she has worked with; those who have tested her methods and improved her strategies and those who have shown her that her philosophy that our children can be both #UNIQUEANDSUCCESSFUL is robust and effective.

There's a well known phrase in Autism circles which says, 'If you've met one child with Autism, you've done just that.' More so than in any other field of education, students with Autism require an individual approach. An approach that taps into their interests, one that teaches them to love learning and above all to believe in themselves.

Victoria believes that as an educator, the most important part of her role is to enable the young people she works with to see their own potential and over the years she's enabled 100s of young people to do just that. Young people who prior to working with her often haven't been able to engage in learning, young people who have been excluded (often from multiple settings) and young people who despite their potential often haven't been able to realise it.

> **Her approach has shown them that they can be #UNIQUEANDSUCCESSFUL.**

And she is passionate about sharing that approach with you. In short she lives, eats and breathes Autism so that you don't have to.